Welcome to Tel

Dear Valued Customer,

We would like to take this opportunity to thank you for purch. some additional information so that you have a wonderful experience. ***Our number one goal is to make sure you get up and running with your new computer!***

Telikin comes with many programs and applications pre-loaded, including Email, Video Chat, Web Browser, Photos, Contacts, Calendar, eReader, etc. If you are relatively new to computers, don't worry. Just take it one step at a time.

Telikin has **Help Videos** for every function. They are accessed using the button. It's near the top right corner of the screen. Just press it, the Help window will open, then press Video to start the video. You can watch and learn at you own pace. Help is always available on the top of your screen. Telikin also comes complete with this, larger print, **User's Manual**. No other computer comes with as much support as Telikin.

Please do not hesitate to call our US-based Customer Support team for any reason – *we're here to help you!* Whether it's learning how to plug in the keyboard or how to create an email account or how to sign up for internet service, we can help.

Our Support number: 1-800-730-6893.
Our Support hours: Mon - Fri 8am-8pm, Sat 10am-6pm, Sun 11:30am-7:30pm, Eastern.

When you turn on your computer, click the "Getting Started" notice to watch your first video tutorial. Read the "Getting Help" chapter in this User Manual to learn more. You can also email our Support Team with any questions by clicking the Help button, and then clicking "Contact Support." (You will need to have email setup to use this feature.)

VIP Support gives you additional valuable features, including priority call answering, automatic backup/restore of your data and special Support Services, including remote access, account setup (email, Facebook and Telichat) and tutorial-based learning. Our Support Team is trained to provide you with the respect you deserve while learning your computer.

Thank you and have fun!

Fred Allegrezza

Fred Allegrezza
CEO Telikin

Call us if you need help, 1-800-730-6893, we're here for you... 7 days a week!

Please read this first

We require that you call us to report any damaged or missing items within 72 hours of delivery.

To take full advantage of your computer, you will need:

- A high-speed Internet connection from an Internet Service Provider (ISP) such as Comcast, Verizon, or CenturyLink.
- An e-mail account including your username and password

If you DO NOT have an Internet connection...

You can proceed with setup but be aware that you will not be able to enjoy the following features until an Internet connection is available:

- Email
- Photo Sharing
- Web Browsing
- Video Chat
- News
- Weather

If you DO have an Internet connection and an e-mail account...

Congratulations! You are only a few steps away from enjoying sharing family photos and surfing your favorite web sites. Please go to Step 1 on page 6.

Cleaning Guidelines

If you wish to clean your computer screen, you can use the enclosed LCD Display Wiper or a dry, clean, lint-free cotton cloth. Or, if you wish to use a liquid cleaner, it must not be ammonia based. Apply the cleaner lightly to a clean, lint-free cloth and then wipe the screen. Do not allow any liquid to drip on the screen.

Caution

You may use commercial keyboard cleaners available at consumer electronics stores. Never pour liquid into the keyboard or immerse the keyboard in any liquid.

Table of Contents

Telikin Quick Start Guide
Step 1: Know the Parts

Back View

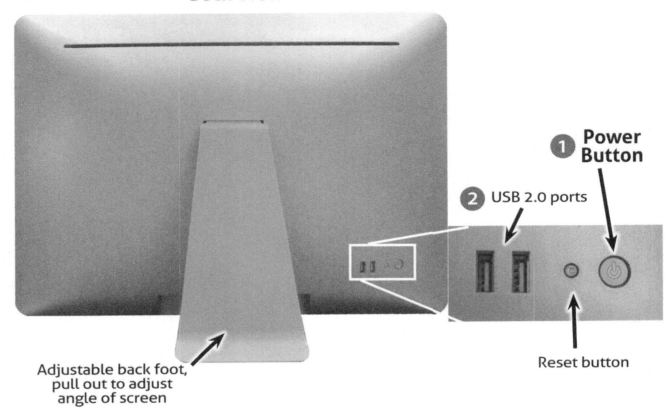

Power Button ①

② USB 2.0 ports

Reset button

Adjustable back foot, pull out to adjust angle of screen

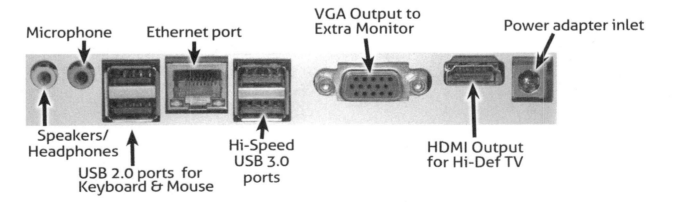

Microphone

Ethernet port

VGA Output to Extra Monitor

Power adapter inlet

Speakers/Headphones

USB 2.0 ports for Keyboard & Mouse

Hi-Speed USB 3.0 ports

HDMI Output for Hi-Def TV

Bottom View

Step 2: Unpack and Prepare your Telikin

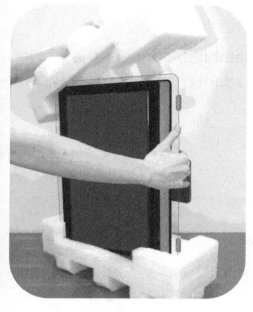

Carefully remove all pieces from the box and place on a flat surface.

Note: The back foot (see page 6) can be adjusted to set the angle of your screen.

Please retain all boxes and packing materials in the event that you need to invoke your warranty.

The factory packaging has been specifically designed and approved by UPS to provide maximum protection during shipping.

The items displayed are included with your computer. **If you are missing any, call Customer Support.**

Touch screen with your finger or the included stylus pointing device

18.6" touchscreen computer

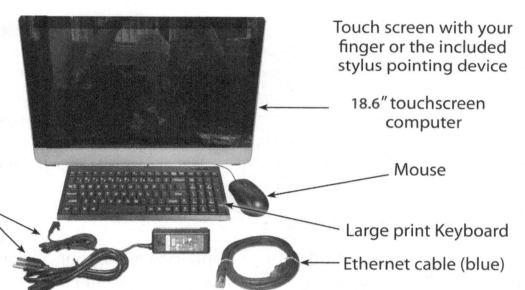

Mouse

Power Supply assembly (these two sections are typically connected together by our team at the warehouse for you).

Large print Keyboard

Ethernet cable (blue)

If using a wired keyboard and mouse, connect them to the USB ports at the bottom of the computer (See page 6 for location).
Look for the plugs with this symbol on them:

Step 3: Connect Power to your Telikin

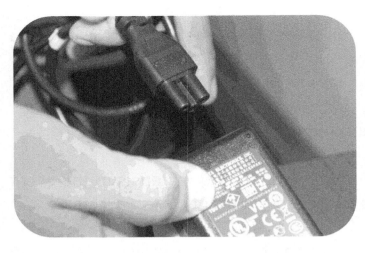

If not already assembled, connect the power cord and power adapter together as shown at left.

Connect the power adapter* to the inlet on the left side of the device (see page 6 for location).

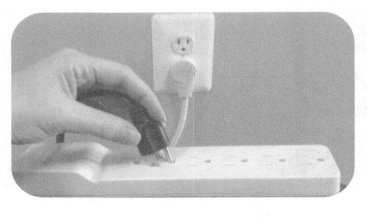

You can plug the power cord into a convenient wall outlet; however, to avoid damage to the computer, it is recommended that you use a UL approved power strip with a surge protector (as shown).

* Use only the supplied adapter to apply power to your Telikin. Using anything other than the supplied adapter could damage your computer.

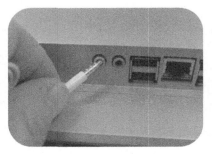

Optional external speakers can be attached to the speaker connector as shown at left. A Microphone connection is available as well.

Step 4: Powering on your Telikin

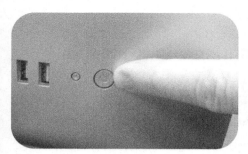

Facing the computer screen, reach around on your left side, to the lower back of the computer. There you'll feel the power button (see page 6 for location), press it to turn on your computer. You can power off the computer by tapping the same power button, or by the preferred method, going to the **Home** screen, click **Settings** then click the **Power Off** button.

There is a light on the front lower left of the computer, indicating power.

Troubleshooting

- If the power indicator is not illuminated, please start by checking the power light indicator on the power adapter connected to the wall outlet (see page 6 for location). Make sure the outlet (or power strip) is not switched off.
- If the light on the power adapter is not illuminated, please make sure the power cord is pushed tightly into the power adapter.
- If the power indicator on the power adapter is illuminated and the power indicator on the front of the device is not, please contact customer support.

Once your Telikin is powered on, you will see the End User License Agreement (EULA). This is an agreement that is customary for software and it states that you agree to only use the software on one computer and not make copies of the software. Please read the EULA and click the box at the bottom left to agree. Once you agree, The EULA will not be shown again, and you will be taken to the **Home** screen.

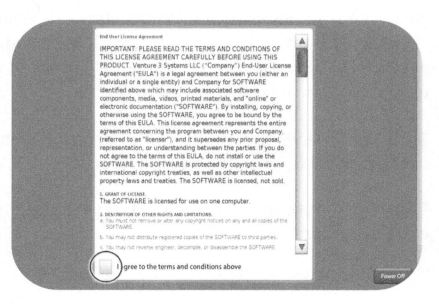

9

Step 5a: Connect to the Internet - Wired

Tech Tip: Calling our support line while the Internet Installation Technician is at your residence will simplify the installation and activation of your internet service.

If you plan to use a wireless (WiFi) Internet connection, continue on to step 5b.

Using the supplied **blue** network cable, connect one end to the network port at the bottom of the computer (see page 6 for location). Connect the other end to the network port of your cable modem or other Internet device.

Note: Before proceedin

g to the next section, make sure your cable modem or other Internet device is powered on.

At this point the Network Status icon 🛜 should light up, indicating that you are connected to the internet. You can find this icon on top of the **Home** screen, just to the right of the time display. You may see this icon: ⊗ , click on either icon to view the Network Status page where you can see what's going on with your setup. If you are using an Ethernet cable to connect to the internet, the **Wired Network** section should show Ethernet **Status** as "Connected."   If this status is "Not Connected," check your wired connections – alternately, if you are using DSL internet service, it may need to be activated. Please call us for help with activation.

Tech Tip: If a wired network connection is available we recommend using it to ensure the best possible computing experience.

Tech Tip: If you need a longer Ethernet cable, you can purchase one at a consumer electronics store.

Step 5b: Connect to the Internet – Wirelessly

In order to connect to the internet wirelessly, you need two things, a modem (typically installed by your Internet Service Provider - ISP) and a wireless router. The wireless router can also be provided by your ISP or obtained at any consumer electronics store. It should be noted that ISPs also may offer a wireless modem, this combines both features into one box. If you are using a separate wireless router, you will need to connect it to the modem using an Ethernet cable, check the router's user manual, then power it on. Now back to your Telikin...

On the **Home** screen, the **Notices** panel will contain a list of items that you can click to easily setup some of your personal information. For now, click the "**Click to set up your Network**" message to view the Network/Internet Settings page.

*You will not see this message if you are already connected to the Internet.

This page displays the status of yours and surrounding networks.

You can also get to the Network/Internet Settings page by clicking **Home**, then click **Settings**, and then click **Network Settings**.

Since you will be using a wireless connection to the internet, take a look at the **Wireless Networks** section. The above

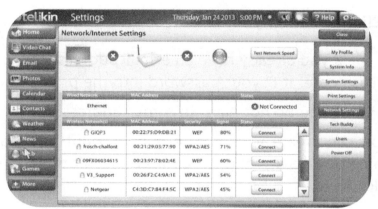

example shows multiple available networks; your setup may only show one. Find your wireless network name in the list and click the **Connect** button for this network in the **Status** column. The name of your wireless network and the password would be provided to you by your installer. If you are installing the router yourself, there are typically two places to check for this information: a) printed on an instruction sheet enclosed with the router, or b) printed directly on the router, typically on the bottom as shown here:

The values you are looking for typically have names like SSID or ESSID, which is the network name. The other value you are interested in is the password, typically called a Key or WEP KEY as shown in the picture to the right:

And here is the name as it appears in the Wireless Networks list. To connect to it, click the **Connect** button to the right. If your network requires a password (there's a padlock to the left of the name), enter it in the **Wireless**

Network Configuration screen and click **Ok, Try to Connect** (the password will be supplied by your internet provider – or may be on the bottom of your modem). Your computer will then attempt to connect to your wireless network. When connected, the status will change to "Connected." Write down your network name and network password on the last page of this book.

Step 6: Configuring your Telikin

On the **Home** screen, the **Notices** panel will contain a list of items that you can click to easily setup some of your personal information. You will see some or all of the following phrases:

"Click to set up your User Profile."

The profile will be used to personalize your Telikin for local weather (by zip code), as well as allow it to maintain your address, birthday, and other contact information for your virtual address book.

Enter your personal information in the text fields given and then click **Save Changes**.

"Click to set up your E-mail account."

- If you already have an e-mail address (i.e., "YourName@gmail.com")...
Please enter it & your password into the provided fields and click **Save**.

- If you do not have an e-mail address...

You can create your own e-mail account using any online service such as Gmail or Hotmail. Once you have your e-mail account information, please enter it into the provided fields and click **Save**.

Write down your e-mail address and password on the last page of this book.

Time Zone Settings

To set your time zone, from the **Home** screen click the **Settings** button, then click the **System Settings** button. If you are not yet connected to the Internet or do not plan to connect to the internet, click the **Set Time** button to set the time manually. Otherwise, select your time zone from the list. Once your computer is connected to the Internet, the exact time will be obtained the next time the computer is turned on.

Congratulations! You have successfully setup your Telikin!

You can now enjoy the easy-to-use, friendly features that will keep you connected to friends and family around the world!

Step 7: Key Usage Features

Volume and Magnification Features

At the top right side of your screen is the Volume button. Click this button to display a bar with a slider. Click and drag the slider up or down to raise or lower the volume level.

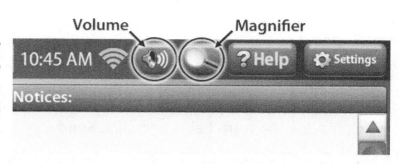

Next to the **Volume** button is the **Magnifier** button. Click this button to open a magnifying window. Move the window to magnify areas of the screen. The cursor is now located in the center of the magnifier window. To disable the magnifier, press the escape (Esc) key on your keyboard, or center the magnifier over the **Magnifier** button and click the button.

Step 8: Documentation and Support

User Manual & Video Tutorials

A copy of this User Manual is also built right into your computer!
To get started, click the **Help** button, located at the top right corner of the screen.

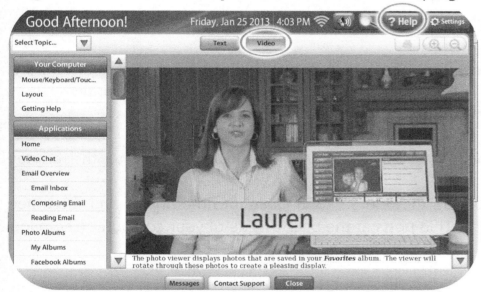

This opens the **Help** window, where you can read or watch video tutorials. It defaults to text descriptions of the page you were viewing when you pushed the Help button.

To watch a video tutorial, click the **Video** button. Click **Text** to return to the written manual.

Also, on the left side is the **Table of Contents**. Click any chapter to instead "go" to that chapter.

Click the **Close** button to close the **Help** window. If you click another blue application button – or any of the settings buttons – and then click the **Help** button again, it will open to that chapter in the manual.

Messages from Us

Occasionally, we will want to share important information with you about your computer. When we do, you'll see this notice on the Home screen: "You have one message from Support." Click this notice to view the message. To re-read a message, or read past messages, click Help, then click Messages.

Email Support

To send an email to Support, please follow these steps:

- Click **Help**
- Click **Contact Support** – this opens an email form
- Complete the form fields and click **Send**

Step 9: Printer Information

In order to ensure an easy "plug and print" experience, we currently only support Hewlett Packard (HP) **inkjet** printers that connect to your computer with a USB cable.

If your computer is connected to the internet, you can easily determine if a particular HP printer is fully compatible.

Check Printer Compatibility

Click **Home**, then click **Settings**, and then click **Print Settings**. Next, click the **Help** button, skip to the **Supported Printers** section that describes how to look up a printer. Call Customer Support if you'd like us to check the compatibility of a specific HP printer model.

Printer Setup

To setup your printer there is no need to install any printer driver software, as HP drivers are already installed on the computer. Follow these steps to connect and install your printer:

- Plug in the power cables, connect to power and turn on the printer
- Load the paper according to the printer instructions
- Open the cartridge door and install the printer cartridges according to the printer instructions
- Close the cartridge door and plug the printer's USB cable into the printer and the other end of the cable into one of the USB ports at the back or side of your computer (see page 6 for location)
- Turn your computer on

Printing a Test Page

From the **Home** screen, click **Settings**, then click **Print Settings** and then click **Print Test Page**.

Step 10: Packing Guidelines

Packing Instructions

Step 1 - Cover the computer with the protective bag.

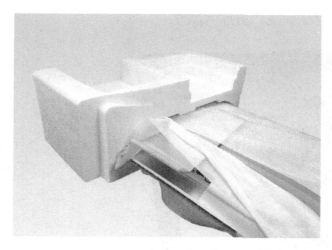

Step 2 - Slide the computer, screen down, into one of the outer foam protectors.

Step 3 - Slide the second foam protector onto the other side of the computer. Then squeeze them together.

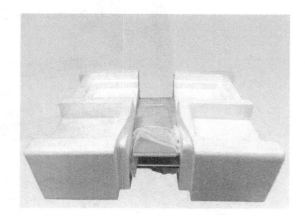

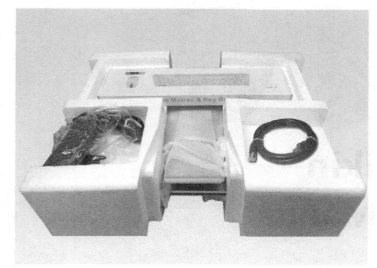

Step 4 - Place the Power Supply and Ethernet cable in the open wells closer to you. Then, place the keyboard and mouse box, with them inside, between the foam protectors as shown.

Step 5 - Slide the foam assembly into the inner box, close it up, and slide it into the outer box.

Step 6 - Close the outer box.

A simpler, easy to use computer.

Telikin
User's Manual

Mouse/Keyboard/Touchscreen

Introduction

Hello and congratulations on the purchase of your computer! In order to control your computer and tell it what to do next, you will need to learn how to use the mouse or touchscreen and the keyboard. In this tutorial, we go over the basic skills of using the mouse, the keyboard and the touch screen, as well as getting help. Let's get started!

We have made this information available to you in a video tutorial. If you would like to watch it, click the Video button at the top of this window. To end the video, click the Text button at the top of this window.

The Mouse

Holding the Mouse

The mouse is a useful device. It fits in the palm of your hand and gives you direct control of your computer screen. The mouse movement directly correlates to the movement of the pointer on the screen (the pointer is shaped like a small triangle). If you move the mouse to the right with your hand, the pointer will also move to the right. If you move the mouse in circles, you will see the pointer move in circles too.

Like any other tool, you'll want to practice using the mouse to get the feel of it and be able to use it comfortably.

To begin using the mouse, lay it on a flat surface close to the right side of the computer. Position the mouse so that the wire facing away from you and plugged into the back or side of the computer. Next, lay your right hand on top of the mouse.

> **Note:** to convert the mouse to left hand use, click the **Settings** button on the top right of the screen, then click the **Mouse Settings** button, then under **Buttons**, select **Left-Handed** and click **Close**. Continue instructions but remember to use left for right.

Its curved shape should fit comfortably in your palm, with your fingers draped down over the front of the mouse toward the wire. The mouse has 2 buttons - a left and a right button, located on the top of the mouse. When you place your right hand on the mouse, your index finger will be on the left mouse button, and your middle finger will be on the right mouse button. You may need to adjust your fingers to position them in this way.

Using the Mouse

You use the mouse to control your computer and tell it what to do next. Using the mouse is a two-step process: first, you move the mouse to position the pointer on the computer screen, and then use your index finger to click the left mouse button. We call this a click because your mouse will make a click sound when you press down on it. From now on we will refer to clicking on the left mouse button as a "click." Clicking on the right mouse button is described below and will be referred to as a "right-click." You may want to practice moving the mouse to see how the pointer on the screen moves with it. Practicing moving the mouse and using the left mouse click with your index finger will help improve your hand-eye coordination.

Mouse Right-Click

For the most part, you will not have to use the button located on the right side of your mouse. Right-clicking is also a two-step process: you position the pointer by moving the mouse and then click down with your middle finger. Right-clicking, as it's called, is used for two functions in your computer: 1) spell correction and 2) saving images.

Spell Correction

Spell correction is available in the Email and Write applications. While typing, if you misspell a word, it will appear with a red squiggly line under it. To correct the misspelled word, simply move the mouse, so the pointer is on top of the misspelled word and click the right mouse button with your middle finger. This will prompt the Spell Check feature, which will open a window with several spelling suggestions. Simply click the checkbox next to the correctly spelled word and then click OK to use it.

Scroll Bars

Often, when you view information on your computer, there may be more pages than will fit on the screen. If you were viewing a book, you would turn the page. On your computer, you will need to "scroll" to see more. To scroll, you will need to learn how to use scroll bars.

Scroll bars are used to move between pages in large documents or websites. Scroll bars can be used to scroll vertically, up and down, through multiple pages, or horizontally, back and forth, across wide pages. Basically, scrolling is used to adjust the viewing area on the screen so you can read and see content that extends beyond the viewing area of your computer screen.

Your computer will sense when there is not enough room to display all the pages or content and display scroll bars automatically on the computer screen.

Using Scroll Bars

Using a scroll bar is a two-step process: first, you position the mouse over the slider - the blue rectangle inside the scrolling area - then you click down and hold the button down while moving the mouse. For vertical scroll bars, you'll move the mouse in an up/down motion. For horizontal scroll bars, you'll move the mouse in a left/right motion. Moving the slider will scroll the document in the direction you move the mouse. You can let go of the mouse button when you have reached the area of the page you want to view.

Scrolling allows you to move quickly through pages. If you want to move one line at a time, click the blue arrow buttons located at the top and bottom of the scroll bar.

The Keyboard

You will use your keyboard whenever typing is required by your computer. The keyboard contains keys marked with letters, numbers, and symbols. When you press a key, the character marked on that key is typed.

Common Keys

Here is an explanation of the most used keys on the keyboard.

1. **Escape** - Used to exit out of Magnification window and other things.
2. **Tab** - Used for indenting - inserts a fixed number of spaces.
3. **Caps Lock** - Turns on or off CAPITALIZATION. When on, a light appears at the top of the keyboard (20). Press Caps Lock again (and another letter) to turn it off.
4. **Shift** - Used in combination with other keys to capitalize letters (Shift with 'A' types capital 'A') and also to access the alternate characters printed on some keys (Shift with '2' types '@').
5. **Control** - Used in combination with other keys to perform special functions.
6. **Speech-to-Text** - Hold down and speak, the computer will type out what you say, for further instructions, see Speech-To-Text on page 19.
7. **Undo** - (2 keys) While holding the Control key (5), tap the 'Z' key to undo typing, or deletion, etc.
8. **Cut** - (2 keys) While holding the Control key (5), tap the 'X' key to cut highlighted text to a scratch pad, later to be 'Pasted.'
9. **Copy** - (2 keys) While holding the Control Key (5), Tap the 'C' key to copy highlighted text
10. **Paste** - (2 keys) While holding the Control Key (5) down, tap the 'V' key to paste copied text to the right of the cursor.
11. **Redo** - (2 keys) While holding the Control key (5), tap the 'Y' key to redo previous **Undo** operations.
12. **Space bar** – adds a space when typing text.
13. **Backspace** - Erases typed characters to the left of the cursor.

14. **Enter** - Inserts a new, blank line. Equivalent to a carriage return on a typewriter.

15. **Arrow Keys** - Used to move the cursor around the screen/document.

16. **Num Lock** – Allows switching between typing of numbers in the Number Keypad (17) or executing the alternate descriptions Home, End, Page Up, Page Down, etc..

17. **Number Keypad** - Allows typing numbers when the Num Lock (16) is on.

18. **Insert** - Switches between Insert and Overtype modes. When entering text, Insert mode adds text, and Overtype mode will type over existing text.

19. **Delete** - Erases typed characters to the right of the cursor.

20. **Caps Lock Light** – Turns on if you are in Caps (CAPITAL letters mode) this will turn off eventually to save battery life.

Keyboard Arrangement

Your keyboard is laid out in the QWERTY format. The name comes from the top row of letters on the keyboard.

The middle section of your keyboard contains letters. Above the letters you will see a row of numbers. The longest key at the bottom of your keyboard is the space bar. This inserts spaces when you are typing. The Enter or Return key is used to insert a new line when moving to the next paragraph.

Shift Key

The shift key is used in combination with other keys to make capital letters and to type symbols on the keyboard. Meaning, you hold down the shift key at the same time you type another key. For example, to type a capital 'G,' press and hold down the shift key with one finger, then press the 'G' key once with another finger.

You may notice some keys have more than one symbol on them - an upper symbol and a lower symbol. When the key is pressed, the lower symbol is what is typed. To get the upper symbol to be typed, you will need to hold down the shift key and then press the key with the symbol once. For example, to type an exclamation point, press and hold down the shift key with one finger, then press the '1' key once with another finger.

Speech-To-Text Key*

If you can't or don't feel like typing then now you don't have to. Here's how:

1. Set the volume on your Telikin to mid-volume or higher (see page: 13 of this manual)

2. Open an email or Write document (you can even open a search window in the web)

3. Press the **Speech-To-Text** button; you will hear a beep, this means the computer is listening.

4. With the button still pressed, speak in a normal speaking voice as clearly as possible, it is best to speak one or two sentences at a time. You will quickly see from experience how well the system works with your voice.

5. When finished with your thought or sentence, release the Speech-To-Text button, you will hear another beep, letting you know the system has stopped listening and will now begin to transcribe what it heard. Please remember, surrounding voices and sounds can interfere with the transcription, so quieter surroundings provide the best results.

*__Speech-To-Text__ requires active VIP subscription.

Backspace Key

When you type, it is not uncommon to make mistakes in spelling. Thankfully there is a button to help you erase mistakes. When you make a mistake, you can press the backspace key. The backspace button is located up and to the right. When you press the backspace key, it will erase one letter back. Pressing Backspace will also remove lines you created by pressing the enter key. If you notice a mistake in the beginning, simply use the arrow keys to move the cursor to where you want to begin erasing, and then press the backspace key.

The Touchscreen

Using the Touchscreen

Your computer has a touchscreen, meaning you can use your finger or the stylus that came with your computer to touch it. The stylus is the small pointing device that looks like a pen. Using the touch screen is very similar to using the mouse, but rather than using the mouse to control the pointer on the screen, you just tap the screen with your finger. If you've never used a mouse, you may find it easier to use the touchscreen. For example, if I want to see the Weather, simply press the Weather button with your finger to GO to the Weather application. You can also use the stylus that came with your computer to touch the screen.

Online User Manual

The Online User Manual is a window that opens when you press the Help button, located at the top right corner of your computer screen. It contains all the information in this User Manual. Clicking Help will display the chapter related to what you are currently doing. To the left of the Help, window is a table of contents. To read any other chapter, simply press on a chapter name and the computer will GO to that chapter. You can watch videos by pressing the Video button at the top of the window. To get back to the written word, press the *Text* button at the top of the window. Also, at the top of the Help window is a droplist that shows you the different sections in the chapter that you are currently reading. Simply press the down arrow to view the list, then, press on a section name to go to it. If the list is long, you can use your scroll bar skills to move up and down in the list. If you have a printer attached to your computer, you can easily print out a chapter to read later by pressing the print button located at the top of this window: 🖨

Screen Layout

Understanding the Screen Layout

Your computer screen is divided into three sections:

- Title Area: this is the area across the top of the screen. It will always remain present. It contains the *Date* and *Time*, the *Network Connection* icon, and the *Volume*, *Help*, and *Settings* buttons.

- Application Buttons: these are the blue buttons along the left side of the screen. These buttons will always remain present. Clicking on an *application button* will go to that application.
- Application Area: this is the large rectangular area to the right of the blue application buttons. This area changes based on what blue button you click.

Title Area
Date and Time

The current date and time are always displayed at the top of the screen. To change your time zone, click Settings, then click System Settings and select your time zone from the droplist.

NOTE: Your computer gets its date and time from the internet. If you are not connected to the internet, your date and time may be off. Once you connect to the internet, your date and time will be corrected. It may take a few minutes for the time to update once you are connected to the internet.

If you are not connected to the internet and want to set the correct time, please do the following:

1. Click Home
2. Click Settings
3. Click System Settings
4. Click Set Time
5. Enter the correct time
6. Click OK

 Network Connection Icon

This icon reflects your network connection status. If all four bars are blue, then you have a strong connection. Each bar that is not blue represents a weaker connection.

TECH TIP: It is a good idea to keep track of this icon, as many of the computer's functions require a strong internet connection.

 Volume Control

To adjust the master volume on your computer, click the *Volume* button and then use your finger or mouse to drag the volume slider bar up & down to increase or decrease the volume.

 Screen Magnifier

After clicking the Screen Magnifier button, a rectangular box will appear around your cursor. This box magnifies whatever it is placed over top of, comparable to using a magnifying glass. You can use this to help read your computer screen easier as well as make selecting links and highlighting text easier. While the Screen Magnifier is active, your cursor will still function normally. To deactivate the Screen Magnifier, click the Magnifier. Alternatively, pressing the **Esc** key on your keyboard will also deactivate the Screen Magnifier.

 Help

This button opens up the **Help** page for the application or feature that you are viewing. The **Help** files are your built-in **User Manual** and feature both Text and Video Tutorials. To learn more about the **Help** files and the benefits of using them, follow these instructions:

1. Click Index, located at the bottom of this window
2. Click *Getting Help*, located in the left-hand panel under the heading **Your Computer**.

When you are done using the Help files, click the red *Close* button located at the bottom of this window.

Settings Button

The *Settings* button allows you to manage simple settings that control the operation of your computer. You may configure your personal user profile in the settings area, as well as set up your email and other accounts.

Application buttons

The application buttons are always visible on the left-hand side of the screen. Simply click an application button to go to that application. Switching between applications is easy too - just click the application button for the application you want to use next!

Home   Brings you to the Home screen, a familiar place to begin.

Video Chat   Allows you to make video and audio calls to all of your Video Chat contacts. For more information on Video Chat, click the *Video Chat* application button, then click *Help*.

Email   Allows you to read, send and manage all your email messages. For more information on Email, click the *Email* application button, then click *Help*

Photos   Allows you to view photos stored on your computer. You can also upload new photos and arrange your photos in albums. This is also where you select the photos for your *Favorites* album. For more information on Photos, click the *Photos* application button, and then click *Help*.

Calendar   Allows you to view the calendar by day, week or month. You can schedule events for birthdays, appointments or holidays and set reminders. For more information on the calendar, click the *Calendar* application button, then click *Help*.

Contacts   Allows you to store and manage your contacts. You can enter addresses, phone numbers, email addresses, birthdays and more. For more information on Contacts, click the *Contacts* application button, and then click *Help*.

Weather   Allows you to view a five day forecast and a Doppler map and get weather for different zip codes. For more information on Weather, click the Weather application button, then click Help.

News   Allows you to view current headlines from a variety of categories and to change your news source. For more information on News, click the *News* application button, then click *Help*.

Web   Allows you to view web pages and bookmark your favorite sites and provides you with a list of quick links to popular sites like Google, eBay, YouTube and more! For more information on the web browser, click the *Web* application button, then click *Help*.

Games   Allows you to play games. Your computer comes preloaded with several games, such as Solitaire, Blackjack and FreeCell. For more information on Games, click the *Games* application button, and then click *Help*.

More   Here you will find more features and tools, such as a timer, a calculator, conversion tools, a word processor and more. For more information, click the *More...* application button, then click *Help*.

Magnification

These magnification buttons allow you to increase or decrease the size of the text. They are available when you are reading email or news, or are browsing the *Web*. Simply click the button with the '+' to increase magnification, or, alternately, click the '-' button to decrease magnification.

NOTE: Scroll bars will also be magnified. This allows you to click them more easily. Also, some content on web pages may not appear when magnification is used. This is due to the design of the web page, not your computer.

? Help Getting Help

Your **User Manual** is built right into your computer! All you have to do is click the **Help** button, located at the top, right corner of your computer screen. Not only can you read the chapters, but you can also watch Video Tutorials.

You may click the **Help** button at any time to learn how to use the applications in your computer. Clicking the Help button will open the Help window to a specific chapter in the user manual. For example, if you click the **Email** button, then click the **Help** button, the user manual will open to the Email chapter. Similarly, if you click the **News** button, then click the **Help** button, the User Manual will open to the News chapter.

Help Window

The Help window appears when you click the **Help** button. A clickable **Table of Contents** is shown on the left and the topic details appear on the right. To switch chapters, click on another chapter in the **Table of Contents**. Drag the blue slider that is located just to the right of the chapter names down to reveal more chapters. In addition to the Table of Contents and Topic Details, there are several helpful buttons:

- **Select Topic...** - This drop down menu allows you to instantly go to any section of the current chapter of the User Manual.
- **Text / Video** - These buttons allow you to switch between a written manual and the video tutorials.
- 🖨 - If you have a printer turned on and connected to the computer, clicking this button will print the page(s), or a portion, see page 116 for more info.
- ⊕ ⊖ - magnification buttons let you increase or decrease the size of the text.
- **Messages** - This button will open a popup window with news and announcements from our Support Team about updates, bug fixes, and new features.
- **Contact Support** - Opens a window that allows you to email questions or report issues to our support team. You must have email working to use this feature.
  - ○ NOTE: Also visible in the Contact Support window are the phone numbers and **wait times for both VIP and Standard support**. This **live view** is provided to help you to choose the best time to call for support. You must have a working internet connection to use this feature.

- **Close** - Closes the Help window.

Video Tutorials

You can watch video tutorials right on your computer! Whenever you click the **Help** button, click the yellow **Video** button to watch a video tutorial. The droplist located at the top, left corner of the Help window shows a list of topics in the tutorial. Click the blue down arrow and then click a topic to skip to that topic in the video or return to a previous topic.

Technical Support

Support Hours

> Monday through Friday, 8am to 8pm, Eastern Time
> Saturdays, 10am to 6pm, Eastern Time
> Sundays, 11:30am to 7:30pm, Eastern Time

Phone Support

Phone Support is a paid service that comes free with your purchase during your trial period. While on the phone, our agents can use a remote access tool to access your computer to assist you. Phone support is available during our regular business hours.

Email Support

If you have an email account configured on your computer, you can send us an email to get help at any time. This is useful if you don't have time to call, or want to contact us outside of business hours. This option is always available to you - even if you're not signed up for our **VIP Service**. To contact our Support Team through email, follow these instructions:

1. Click **Help**
2. Click **Contact Support** - this will open an email form
3. Complete the fields in the form (use the blue down arrow to select a Feature area)
4. Click **Send**

This will send an email to our Support Team and create a support ticket. You will first receive an automated response in your email inbox with your ticket number. Next you will receive a personal email response from our Support Team during regular business hours.

# Home

The Home screen, as its name implies, is a familiar place to begin. It will always be displayed when you turn on your computer and will provide you with a quick overview of what's happening in your world.

From the Home screen, you will be able to log in to your account, access all the features of your computer and view important notices.

To get to the Home Screen, click the Home button.

When you click the Home button, the application area will show a Photo Viewer, a Notices board and several Widgets.

Notices	The Notices board displays events that need your attention. Types of notifications include Software Updates, new email messages, new contact information, missed video chat calls, or calendar event reminders. Clicking a notice will allow you to take action on the notice. For example, clicking on a notice that informs you of new emails will take you to your email inbox. Similarly, clicking a new Software Update notice will prompt you to restart your computer to complete the update.
Photo Viewer	The photo viewer displays photos that are saved in your Favorites album. The viewer will rotate through these photos to create a pleasing display.
Widgets	The Home screen contains small information boxes, called widgets. These widgets give you a brief overview of information. Clicking a widget will give you more detailed information.
News Widget	Shows a sub-set of the top stories from your choice of new sources. Click a headline in the News widget to see the full story.
Weather Widget	Shows a concise view of current and pending weather conditions. Click the Weather widget to see a live Doppler radar map of the weather in your area as well as a full 5-day forecast.

Quotes & Trivia Widget	Shows random quotes or trivia questions for your enjoyment. A new quote or trivia question will be shown each time you return to the home page. You can also click the Quotes or Trivia tab to bring up a new quote or trivia question.

Logging In

Login Button

If you have created user accounts on your computer, when you turn on the computer you will see a green Login button near the top right corner of the screen. If you have not created any user accounts, then you will not see the Login button.

To login, do one of the following:

- If only one user account has been created, and you **do not have** a password defined for this account, simply click Login.

- If only one user account has been created, and you do have a password defined for this account, enter your password, and then click Login.

- If multiple user accounts have been configured, select your username from the droplist, enter your password (if one is defined), and then click Login. If you are the Primary user, there will be a star next to your username that will always be displayed at the top of the droplist.

Guest Mode

When you have created user accounts and have not logged in yet, the computer is in Guest Mode. You may still use the computer in Guest Mode, but with limited functionality. Guest Mode adds a level of privacy and security to your computer that is useful when you would like guests or children to be able to use your computer, but not be able to see your email or your contacts or other private information.

Features that can be used in Guest Mode:

- Home - access to the Home screen
- Weather
- News
- Web - surfing the internet
- Games
- More - helpful tools

Video Chat

Video Chat allows you to send and receive free video and audio calls to friends and family across the globe.

Internet Connection

In order to use Video chat, you must be connected to the Internet. To determine if you are connected to the Internet, look for the network connection icon: 📶 at the top of your screen. It should display at least one blue bar. If there are no blue bars, then you are not connected to the internet. Click the network connection icon to manage your network connection.

Tech Tip: The network connection icon represents the strength of your computer's connection to your network not necessarily to the internet; therefore if you have one or more blue bars and are not able to access Video Chat, check your Network/Internet Settings page by clicking on the network connection icon as you may be encountering an issue with your internet connection.

Telichat Overview

Telichat is a Video Chat service that we developed to integrate seamlessly with your computer, while still being accessible to your family and friends on other computers, tablets, and smartphones.

In order to make Video Chat calls with Telichat both you and the person(s) you wish to call:

- Must have a Telichat Account.

- Must sign into Telichat.

o   If you already have a Telichat Account set up on this computer, then clicking on Video Chat will automatically log you in.

o   Instructions for creating a Telichat account are below.

Configure Video Chat with Telichat

Creating a Telichat Account

Creating a Telichat account is very easy to set up for both you and your family & friends. Below are the instructions for creating a Telichat account.

Creating your Telichat Account

If you have an email address set up on your computer, simply click Video Chat to automatically create a Telichat account. This account will be linked to your computer so that it can only be accessed from your computer. This account will automatically link to your Contacts application.

Note: If you wish to access your Telichat account from another computer, tablet, or smartphone, follow the instructions listed in the Resetting your Password section below.

Creating a Telichat Account on a different computer, tablet, or smartphone*

1.   Open your web browser (i.e. Chrome, Firefox, Safari, Edge, etc.).

2.   Go to https://chat.telikin.com

3.   Click on the Login / Register button at the top right-hand corner of the page.

o   This will take you to the Telichat Login page.

4.   Click on the Register tab on the left side on the page.

5.   Type your first name in the First Name field.

6.   Type your last name in the Last Name field.

7.   In the Username field, create a unique username between 5 - 12 characters long.

8.   Type your email address in the Email field.

9.   In the Password field, create a password for your account that is at least 8 characters long.

Note: Passwords are case-sensitive. This means that a capital letter and a lowercase are seen as different characters even if they are the same letter. For example: if your password was Apples1234 and you entered apples1234, then the computer would see this as an incorrect password.

10.   Type the same password again in the Retype Password field.

11.   Click Register.

At this time, Telichat is not supported by iPhones and iPads.

Signing in to Telichat

If you are signing in to Telichat on your computer, simply clicking Video Chat will automatically log you in to your account. If you are signing in to Telichat on a different computer, tablet, or smartphone, follow the instructions below.

Signing in to Telichat on a different computer, tablet, or smartphone*

1.   Open your web browser (i.e. Chrome, Firefox, Safari, Edge, etc.).

2.   Go to https://chat.telikin.com

3.   Click on the Login / Register button at the top right-hand corner of the page.

o   This will take you to the Telichat Login page.

4.   Type either your Telichat username or email address in the Username or email field.

5.   Type your password in the Password field.

o   If you cannot remember your password or do not have a password, you can reset it by following the instructions in the Resetting your Password section below.

6.   Click Login.

Resetting your Password

If you are trying to sign in to your Telichat account but cannot remember your password, following the steps below will allow you to reset your password.

1.   Open your web browser (i.e. Chrome, Firefox, Safari, Edge, etc.).

2.   Go to https://chat.telikin.com

3.	Click on the Login / Register button at the top right-hand corner of the page.

o	This will take you to the Telichat Login page.

4.	Type your email address in the Username or email field.

5.	Click Forget Password.

o	This will send you an email with a link to reset your password.

6.	Check your email to see if you received the Telichat password reset email.

o	The email will be sent from noreply@telikin.com. If you do not see the email after a decent amount of time, check your Spam folder in case it was accidentally flagged as spam.

7.	Open the Telichat password reset email.

8.	Click on the password reset link.

9.	In the Password field, create a password for your account that is at least 8 characters long.

Note: Passwords are case-sensitive. This means that a capital letter and a lowercase are seen as different characters even if they are the same letter. For example: if your password was Apples1234 and you entered apples1234, then the computer would see this as an incorrect password.

10.	Type the same password again in the Retype Password field.

11.	Click Change Password.

Setting a Password for an Automatically Generated Account

If you want to use your automatically generated Telichat account on a different computer, tablet or smartphone, you will first need to create a password by following these steps:

1.	Go to Video Chat.

2.	Click on your name in the upper right-hand corner.

3.	Click the Logout button on the My Account drop down menu.

4.	Go to Web.

5.	Click in the URL bar located at top of the screen between the Add Bookmark ( ) button and the green Go button.

6.	If there is already something typed in the URL bar, erase it using the backspace key on your keyboard. If the URL bar is empty, skip this step.

7.	Type chat.telikin.com/app/auth

8.	Press Enter on your keyboard or click on the green Go button.

9.	Type your email address in the Username or email field.

10.	Click Forget Password.

o	This will send you an email with a link to reset your password.

11.	Go to Email.

12.	Check your email to see if you received the Telichat password reset email.

o	The email will be sent from noreply@telikin.com. If you do not see the email after a decent amount of time, check your Spam folder in case it was accidentally flagged as spam.

13. Open the Telichat password reset email.

14. Click on the password reset link.

15. In the Password field, create a password for your account that is at least 8 characters long.

Note: Passwords are case-sensitive. This means that a capital letter and a lowercase are seen as different characters even if they are the same letter. For example: if your password was Apples1234 and you entered apples1234, then the computer would see this as an incorrect password.

16. Type the same password again in the Retype Password field.

17. Click Change Password.

Understanding Telichat Contacts

Contacts List

On the right side of the screen is your Contacts list, which lists all of your contacts alphabetically by last name. To the left of the Contacts list are Alphabetic Tabs, which allow you to quickly navigate through your list. For example, if you have a contact with the last name "Miller", click the M-N tab

M-N .Alternatively, you can scroll through your Contacts list using the scroll up ( ) and scroll down ( ) arrows, which are located at the top and bottom of the Alphabetic Tabs respectively.

Adding a Contact

To add a new contact, follow these steps:

1. Click Video Chat.

2. Click New Contact, located at the top of the Contacts list.

3. Type the contact's first name in the First Name field.

4. Type the contact's last name in the Last Name field.

5. Type the contact's email address in the Email field.

o Click Update to add the contact.

o If you change your mind and no longer wish to add the contact, click Cancel.

Note: if you are using Telichat on your computer, the new contact will be automatically added to your Address Book in the Contacts app.

Invite a Contact

If you add a contact and they do not have a Telichat account, you can send them an email invitation to join Telichat. To invite a contact to join Telichat, follow these steps:

1. Click Video Chat.

2. Click on the contact in your Contacts list.

3. Click Invite ( ).

4. A popup will appear asking you if you would like to email an invitation to your contact.

o Click Send Invite to send them an email invitation.

o If you change your mind and no longer wish to send the contact an invite, click Cancel.

Edit a Contact

You can edit an existing contact by clicking on the contact's name in the Contacts list, then pressing Edit ( ). After pressing Edit, you can change the contact's first name, last name, or email address. When you are satisfied with your changes, press Update. If you change your mind and no longer wish to edit the contact, click Cancel.

Remove a Contact

If you want to remove a contact from your Contacts list, simply click on the contact's name then click Remove ( ). A prompt will appear asking if you are sure you want to remove your contact. Click OK to remove the contact; however if you no longer wish to remove the contact, click Cancel.

Send a Message

If you want to get a hold of a contact but they are offline or already on a call, you can send them a message by following these steps:

1.   Click Video Chat.

2.   Click on the contact in your Contacts list.

3.   Click Send Message ( ).

4.   A popup will appear telling you to send a brief message to your contact.

5.   Click in the Enter message... field and type your message.

o   Click OK to send the message.

o   If you no longer want to send your message, click Cancel.

6.   If you clicked OK, your message will be sent to your contact as an email. If they use Telichat on an Android smartphone or tablet, they will also receive a push notification* on their device.

*If the contact did not enable push notifications for Telichat, then they will only receive an email.

Contact Status

To the left on each contact you will see their status to let you know if they are available to call or not. Below is a list of each status an explanation of what it means.

- 　　　- This means that the contact is logged in to Telichat and not currently on a call.

- 　　　- This means that the contact is logged in to Telichat and currently on a call.

- 　　　- This means that the contact is not logged in to Telichat.

- 　　If you do not see a Contact Status for a contact, then they do not have a Telichat account. You can invite them to join Telichat using the instructions in the Invite a Contact section above.

Using Telichat
Make a Video Call

You will only be able to make a video calls to contacts that are online. To make a video call, follow these steps:

1.   Click Video Chat.

2.   Click on the contact in your Contacts list that you want to call.

3.   Click Call ( ).

4.   A prompt will appear asking you if you want to call the selected contact.

o   Click Yes to call the selected contact.

o   If you no longer want to call the selected contact, click Cancel.

When the person you are calling answers, you will see them in the active video window. You will also see yourself in the top right-hand corner of their video, this is called your video thumbnail.

Start a Group Video Call

On Telichat you can have more than one contact in a call at a time; this is called a group video call. To start a group video call, follow these steps:

1.   Click Video Chat.

2.   Click on the first contact in your Contacts list that you want to call.

3.   Click Call ( ).

4.   A prompt will appear asking you if you want to call the selected contact.

5.   Click Yes to call the selected contact.

6.   When the person you are calling answers, you will see them in the active video window and yourself in the top right-hand corner of their video, this is called your video thumbnail.

7.   Click on the next contact in your Contacts list that you want add to the group video call.

8.   Click Call.

9.   A prompt will appear asking you if you want to call the selected contact.

10.   Click Yes to call the selected contact.

11.   When this contact answers, they will be added to your current video call. You will see their video thumbnail appear below yours in the top right-hand corner of the active video window.

12.   Repeat steps 7-11 until you have added everyone you want to the group video call.

Receive a Video Call

When someone is calling you on Telichat, the computer will ring and display a popup letting you know who is calling. If you want to accept their video call, click Answer. If you do not want to answer the call, click Decline. If you are using Telichat on your computer, clicking Answer will automatically take you to the Video Chat application if you are not currently there.

Changing the Active Video

When you are in a video call or group video call, the first contact you called is set as the active video. You can change the active video by clicking another participant's video thumbnail. The video thumbnail for the current active video is darkened so that you can easily determine whose video you are watching.

Video Quality

In the top right-hand corner next your video thumbnail is the video quality icon, which will display HD, SD, LD, or AUD.

•   HD - This means that the video is currently being displayed in High Definition.

•   SD - This means that the video is currently being displayed in Standard Definition.

•   LD - This means that the video is currently being displayed in Low Definition.

•   AUD - This means that the contact in the active video window either does not have a web cam or it is disabled.

End a Video Call

When you are done talking to your contact(s) and want to end the call, you can click the Leave ( ) button, located in the center of the video toolbar. Alternatively you can click Hang Up ( ), located below the active video window.

Understanding the Video Toolbar

The video toolbar appears when you are on a video call and move your cursor on top of the active video window. It contains several useful functions, which are detailed below.

Open / Close Chat

While you are on a video call, you can send chat messages to you the other participants in the call as well. To open the text chat window, click the Open Chat ( ) button, which is located on the far left of the video toolbar. Once the chat window is open, type what you want to say and press Enter on your keyboard. You can also add some fun emojis to your message by clicking on the emoji ( ) button and selecting an emoji. To close the text chat window, click on the Open Chat button again.

Mute / Unmute

You can mute the outgoing sound during a call by clicking the Mute button ( ). The contact(s) you are speaking with via Telichat will no longer be able to hear you. When the call is muted, the Mute button will change to an Unmute button ( ). Clicking Unmute will allow the contact(s) you are speaking with via Telichat to hear you again. These buttons are located near the center of the video toolbar to the left of the Leave button.

Start / Stop Camera

While in a video call, you can turn your web cam off by using the Stop Camera button ( ). When the web cam is turned off, then the other participant(s) of the call will only be able to hear you, and the Stop Camera button will change to an Start Camera button ( ). Clicking Start Camera will allow the other participant(s) of the call to see you again. By default your web cam will be on at the beginning of the call. These buttons are located near the center of the video toolbar to the right of the Leave button..

More Actions

The More Actions ( ) button, which is located on the far right of the video toolbar, allows you to access additional features, such as full screen mode.

Email

Email stands for "electronic mail". In order to use email, you will need to have an email account and a working internet connection.

Your Email Inbox

It is a good idea to keep your inbox organized. Just like your regular mail, you'll want to read your emails daily and delete unwanted or old emails (similar to throwing away junk mail). You can also organize your inbox by moving important emails to folders.

To view the email inbox, click the Email button.

Understanding the Inbox

The inbox is a list of all the email messages you have received. Email is sorted by date, with the most recent email at the top of the list. For each email in the list, you will see the subject whether or not it has attachments, the sender and the date it was sent.

Subject

The subject of the email is displayed in this column.

Attachments

If you see this icon in the column, it means that the email message has one or more attachments.

Replied

If you see this icon in the column, it means that you replied to this email at some point. It's a way to help you keep track of the email that you have replied to.

From

The sender of the email is displayed in this column.

Date

This column displays the date the email was sent.

Checkbox

The checkbox is used to select several emails at once. This is convenient for moving or deleting several emails.

Creating, Reading, and Forwarding an Email

Create an Email

To create an email, click the Email button, and then click Compose Email. This will open a new email message. Click Help when viewing the new email message to get more information on how to address, compose and send your email.

Read an Email

To read an email, just click the Email button and then click the subject line of the email or click in the checkbox (the square on the same line) and then click the **Read** button on the right. This will open the email so you can read it.

Forward an Email

You may forward an email you have received to one or more people in your contacts list. To forward an email, click the email you wish to forward. Clicking on the subject line of the email will open it as if you wanted to read it. Then click the Forward button on the right-hand side of the screen. The Compose Email screen will be brought up so that you can fill in the To: and CC: fields. You can also attach files and type a message in the body. When you are satisfied with your message, press the Send button.

Managing Email

Delete Email

You can organize your emails by deleting unwanted or old emails. Click the check box next to the email(s) you want to delete and then click Delete. You will be asked to confirm your decision.

Move Email

You can organize your emails by moving them to different folders. Click the check box next to the email(s) you want to move and then click Move... You will then be prompted to select the destination folder. Click the destination folder, and then click Ok.

Find an Email

Click the Find... button to initiate a search for emails based on a word or a phrase in the email. To find email, follow these instructions:

1. Click Find...

2. Enter the word(s) to search for
3. Click Ok
4. A list of emails containing the search word(s) will appear.
5. To cancel the search and see your inbox again, click Clear Search.

Refresh Mail

The computer checks for new email automatically every 15 minutes. Clicking "Refresh Mail" makes this happen immediately.

Folders

Folders are used to organize and store your emails. You can move important emails into folders to store them for later reference. To view a different folder, click the folder name. The most commonly used folders are:

Inbox Folder

All new emails go into your inbox. Click Inbox to view emails in the Inbox.

Sent Folder

All sent emails go into your sent folder. Click Sent to view emails in the Sent folder.

Drafts Folder

Emails that you are working on and save for later will be saved to this folder. Click Drafts to view emails that have been saved to the Drafts folder.

Trash

When you delete an email, it is moved to the Trash folder. An email that has been deleted will remain in the Trash folder for 30 days before it is permanently deleted. To remove an email from the Trash folder, perform the following steps:

1. Click Trash
2. Find the email(s) that you want to remove from the Trash
3. Click the checkbox(es) to the left of the email(s)
4. Click Move...
5. Click the destination folder
6. Click Ok

Other Folders

In addition to the commonly used folders, you can create other folders to manage your emails. To create new folders, simply click Email, and then click Settings. Please see the Managing Folders section below for more detailed information on managing folders. If you configure your computer with an existing email account that has folders, those folders will be imported.

Managing Folders

To create, rename or delete folders, simply click Email, click Settings, and then click Folders. On this page, you will see a list of your existing folders. If you have more folders than are visible on one page, a scroll bar will appear to the right to allow you to scroll through your folder list.

NOTE: Folders will be synchronized between the computer and the mail server only for email accounts configured with IMAP.

To create a folder, simply click Add, enter a name for your new folder, and then click OK.

To rename a folder, click the checkbox to the left of the folder name and then click Rename. Enter a new name for the folder and then click OK.

To delete a folder, click the checkbox to the left of the folder name and then click Remove. If you click OK, this will remove the folder and all the emails in it.

Composing an Email

This screen allows you to compose, address and send your email message, as well as add or remove attachments.

Emails are composed of three parts: the header, the toolbar, and the message body.
- The header is the gray area at the top of the email. When composing new email, this is where you address your email, give the email a subject, and view attached files.
- The toolbar is located below the header and consists of several buttons and dropdowns that allow you to change the formatting of the text in the body of the email.
- The message body is the large white area below the toolbar, where you type your actual email message.

TO:

This field lists the recipients of the email. Like a letter, an email must have a recipient, unlike a letter, you can send a single email to multiple recipients at the same time. You can specify recipients a few different ways. If your recipient's email information is already in your Contacts list, you have two options:
1. Click in the white box to the right of the green To: button, then start typing in the person's name or email address. Your computer will make suggestions, showing the contact that matches what you've typed up to that point. These suggestions are shown in alphabetical order, once you are satisfied that the suggestion matches your intended recipient, you can press Enter on your keyboard. The name of the

recipient will then be displayed. You can enter multiple recipients, but you must press Enter after every entry.

2. Click on the green To: button, your list of Contacts will be displayed, select one or more intended recipients then click the green OK button on the bottom. Your recipient(s) names will be shown in the To: window.

* **Note**: If you select a contact that has more than one email in your Contacts list, the email will be sent to the address listed as Email 1 in their Contact information.

For recipients not in your Contacts list, you can also enter their email address manually, just click in the white box to the right of the green To: button, then type in the email address.

Each email address can easily be removed from the message by clicking the green circle ⊖ behind that name. If the circle is red ⊖ then the address that has been entered is neither a contact of yours nor is it entered in a proper email address format.

CC:

"CC" stands for "Carbon Copy", a term dating back to when a typist would duplicate pages by sandwiching carbon paper with extra sheets in the typewriter. This field is similar to the To: field, you can specify recipients who will receive a copy of the email in the same two ways, see above. Normally email is sent using the To: option, and use the CC: option to send a copy of an email to people you want to read, but not necessarily reply to it. The BCC: field is enabled by default, but can be disabled in the Email Settings

BCC:

"BCC" stands for "Blind Carbon Copy. Email recipients entered into the BCC: field will receive a copy of the email; however, their email addresses will be concealed from all other recipients. You can add recipients to the BCC: field in the same ways as the To: and CC: fields. The BCC: field is disabled by default, but can be enabled in the Email Settings

Subject:

Click in the field to the right of the word Subject: to enter a subject for the email. This gives the recipient an idea of what the email is about. An example of a subject might be "Want to meet for lunch?"

 **Zoom In/Out**

Located to the right of the subject, these buttons allow you to increase or decrease the size you view the text of email message body at to make it easier to read. Changing the text size in this way does not affect how the email looks to recipient of the email.

 On Screen Keyboard

The On-Screen Keyboard is a digital keyboard that will normally appear on your screen when you click into a typeable field while not having a physical keyboard connected to the computer. If you have the On-Screen Keyboard set to auto with the physical keyboard unplugged or have the On-Screen Keyboard set to always be available, clicking this button will bring up the On-Screen Keyboard. When the On-Screen Keyboard is active, pushing this button again will disable the On-Screen Keyboard. This button will not be available if you have the On-Screen Keyboard set to auto with the physical keyboard plugged in or have the On-Screen Keyboard set to never be available.

Tech Tip: You can change the On-Screen Keyboard settings via the drop-down menu on the System Settings page.

Attachments:

If you attach one or more files to an email, the Attachments list will appear on the right side of the heading. This area lists all lists all of the files attached to the email. Clicking on the name of a file in the Attachments list will allow you to view it. If you wish to remove the file from the email, click Remove. You can print an attachment by clicking the Print button at the bottom. If you wish to view a different attachment, you can use the Previous and Next buttons to do so without having to go back to the list. When you are finished viewing the attachments, click Close.

The Toolbar

The toolbar is located below the header and consists of several buttons and dropdowns that allow you to change the formatting of the text in the body of the email. If you push a button before typing, it will change the formatting on all of the text you type after pushing it. To change the formatting of existing text, simply highlight the text and push the button in the toolbar for the formatting you want use. Below is a list of all of the toolbar buttons and their functions.

 Creates **bold text**.

I Creates *italicized text*.

U Creates <u>underlined text</u>.

≡ Creates text aligned with the left margin of the page.

≡ Creates text that is centered in the page.

≡ Creates text that is aligned with the right margin of the page.

☺ **Insert Emoji**

This button allows you to insert emojis into your email. An emoji is a small image or icon

that you can use to express an idea or emotion. For instance you can use 😮 to

convey that you are surprised or you can use 🎂 to help wish someone a Happy
Birthday.

Font

Click the Font dropdown list to display a list of font types. Select the font you like, and
the text you type will be in that font.

Size

Click the Size dropdown list to display a list of font sizes. Select a size you like, and the
text you type will be in that size. Unlike the zoom in and out buttons, which are located
in the heading, changing the font size through the Size droplist, will show on the
recipients end as well.

 Font Color

This button allows you to change the color of the font, such as green, purple, teal, and
many more. Clicking this button will display a dropdown menu with 20 colors to choose
from.

Background Color

This button allows you to change the color behind the text, such
as gold, magenta, orange, and many more. Clicking this button will display a dropdown
menu with 20 colors to choose from.

The Message Body

The message body is the large white area below the toolbar, where you type your actual email message. This is the actual email message. To begin, click in the message body, a blinking cursor to appear. The cursor is the insertion point where typing will begin - it's like putting a pencil down on paper. Once you have typed your email and are ready to send it, click Send. When the recipient responds to you, the email body will contain their response. The body keeps all the communication in one place, so you can read through the conversation.

Spell Check

When you are composing an email, you might notice that occasionally words are underlined with a jagged red line. This means that these words may be misspelled. You can right-click the underlined word to see possible corrections. Please be aware that the red line does not necessarily mean that a word IS misspelled but rather that it is not recognized by the computer. A common example of this is a person's last name.

Email Functions
Print

If you have a printer plugged into your computer, clicking the Print button will generate a Print Preview popup. The left side of this popup shows how the print out will look, while the right side of this popup lets you choose a printer to use, the number of copies you wish to print, and a page range (if there is more than one page). When you have selected your options, click the green Print button to print your email. Alternatively, you can save the print preview as a PDF file by clicking the green Save PDF, or exit the Print Preview screen by clicking the red Close button.

Send

Clicking the Send button sends the current email to the recipients listed in the To: field, as well as the CC: and BCC: fields, if enabled.

Save Draft

Clicking the Save Draft button saves the current email in the Drafts folder, so that you can come back to it later without having to send it. You may wish to do this if you don't have the email address of the person you wish to send the email to or just as a precaution. The draft will stay in the Drafts folder until the email is sent.

Delete

Clicking the Delete button cancels the new email and returns to the Inbox. A popup will appear giving you the following three options on how to proceed:

- Clicking Save to Drafts will save a draft of the email you are composing prior to exiting the Compose Email screen.
- Clicking Delete will delete the email you are composing and exit the Compose Email screen.
- Clicking Cancel will close the popup and take you back to the email you are composing.

Attach File

Click this button to add photos, documents or other files as attachments. When you click Attach File, you will be presented with a series of windows that will guide you through selecting what files you want to send along with the email. To one or more files to an email, follow these steps:

1. Click the Attach File... button, located below the Delete button on the right side of the screen.
2. Click on the folder that contains the type of file you want to attach. For example, if you want to attach a photo, click on the Photos folder.
3. Click on the folder or album that contains the file(s) you want to attach. If the file(s) you want to attach are not in a folder, skip this step.
4. Select the file(s) you want to send by clicking the check box next to each file.
5. Once all the files you want to send are selected, click the green Attach button, located at the bottom of the window.
6. If there are files in other folders that you want to attach to the same email, repeat steps 1-5.

NOTE: Email Providers typically limit the size of an email. For that reason, if you are attaching photos larger than 500kb, you will be given the option to reduce the file size of those photos (to one better optimized for sending through e-mail). This is to help in sending multiple photos in a single email.

Keyboard Controls

Functions like Cut, Copy, Paste, Undo and Redo, can be utilized by using a combination of keystrokes. To Cut or Copy, simply highlight the text you wish to duplicate. Then:

- Simultaneously press ctrl, located in the bottom left corner of your keyboard, and C, if you want to Copy the text.
- Simultaneously press ctrl and X, if you want to Cut the text.

To Paste text that you have copied or cut, simply click where you would like to place the text, then simultaneously press ctrl and V.

The Undo function can remove typed words or sentences (or undo the removing of them) when you simultaneously press ctrl and Z , doing so multiple times can undo multiple entries, undoing more typing (or deleting) with each attempt. The Redo function similarly works when you simultaneously press ctrl and Y , this is the equivalent of undoing the last Undo.

Note: Keyboard Controls can only be utilized by using a real keyboard; the on-screen keyboard will not work.

Reading an Email

This screen shows an individual email message.

To read email:

- **Click the Email button**
- **Click the words of the Subject of an individual email**

Email Message

Message Header

The message header is the gray area at the top the email. It represents the "envelope" of the email. The header displays the timestamp (date and time) the email was received/sent, the subject of the email, the sender/receiver and any attachments that may have been sent with the email.

Message Body

The message body is the white area below the header. This is the actual email message. This is where the email conversation is displayed. Use the blue scroll bars to scroll through the conversation. If the body contains any web links, clicking on a link will open a popup window displaying the website. Click the Close button to close the popup window. You can use the zoom buttons (see below) to increase or decrease the size of the text displayed in the message body.

Email Attachments

Email attachments are files that are sent with the email. There are many kinds of attachments. Examples of attachments are images, documents, contact information, spreadsheets, videos, music, or calendar events.

Currently, you may view images, documents (Word compatible documents or PDF files), contact information, videos, music, and calendar events. You are able to save unsupported file types; however, you will not be able to view these files at this time. You will be able to view these files in the near future.

Viewing Email Attachments

You can view attachments directly from the email by clicking View Attachments. The attachment will open in a viewing window. Click the Close button to close it.

If the attachment you are viewing is a **video** or **audio** file, you can view / listen to that file directly in the view attachments popup.

If the attachment you received is **Contact Information**, then it will automatically be saved and added to your contact list. If the contact is already in your contact list, then any information that is new will be added to that contact; however if there is information that would overwrite previously saved information, then you must view the attachment and save it manually to confirm the change. For example, Let's say John Doe is in your address book with just his name, email address, and phone number, so he sends you his contact information by email that includes his current home address, but a new phone number. When you open his email, you will see a dialog box that says "Contact information saved" and his home address will be added to your address book; however in order to save his new phone number you must view the attachment and click Save.

Saving Email Attachments

When you view the attachments, you will also have the option to save them to your computer. To save an attachment, click the **Save** button. If you are saving a document, the File Manager will open where you can select (by clicking on) a destination folder. If you are saving an image, you will be prompted to save it to one of your albums.
To view your saved documents, use the File Manager, accessible by clicking the More button. To view your saved images, click the Photos to view your albums.

Email Message Functions

Zoom In/Out - Increase or decrease the size of the email.

Print - If you have a printer plugged into your computer, clicking the print button will open a **Print Request** popup. By default this will print one copy of your full email, but you can customize the orientation of your paper and the number of copies you wish to print. You can also print just a portion of the message (to save paper) by highlighting that section and checking the **Print Selection Only?** checkbox. When you have selected your options, click the green **Print** button to print your email.

Text to Speech Click this button to have the computer read an email to you! Make sure your volume control is set to a comfortable level. Click it again or close the email to stop.

CC: Clicking the green button after other CC'd recipient's names allows you to add their info to your address book by either creating a new contact or updating an existing contact.

TO: Clicking the green button after other recipient's names allows you to add their info to your address book by either creating a new contact or updating an existing contact.

From:

Clicking the green button after the sender's name allows you to add their info to your address book by either creating a new contact or updating an existing contact.

Reply/Reply All:

Clicking this button will bring up a dialog box asking if you want to **Reply to Sender** or **All recipients**. Replying to Sender will allow you to write an email to the person who wrote the email to which you are replying, while Replying to All recipients will send it to everyone who received the original email as well as the sender.

TECH TIP: If you want to reply to some but not all of the recipients then:

1. Click the Reply.
2. Click All.
3. When your reply email opens, remove the email addresses of those that you do not wish to send the message to.

Forward:

Forwarding an email sends an email you have received to one or more people in your contacts list. To forward an email, click the Forward button on the right-hand side of the screen. The Compose Email screen will be brought up so that you can fill in the To: and CC: fields. You can also attach files and type a message in the body. When you are satisfied with your message, press Send.

Delete

Deletes the current email. You will be asked to confirm this decision.

Move...

Moves the current email to a different folder. This is very helpful when organizing your emails. A pop-up window will appear asking you to select a destination folder.

Email Navigation Functions

Next   Shows the next email in the list.
Previous   Shows the previous email in the list.
Back to Inbox   Returns you to the Inbox. This button reflects your current folder. For example, if you are viewing sent items, this button will change to Back to Sent Mail.

 # Photos

Photos lets you easily view, manage and upload digital photos.

To view photos, click the Photos button.

The Photos application lets you store and view digital photos on your computer and organize them into albums. You can upload photos to your computer directly from your camera, camera card or external storage device.

Albums

The Photos application uses the concept of **albums** to group your photos. Just like a real photo album, you can add or remove photos from these albums. Albums that contain photos which are stored on the computer display with a **blue** binding.

Favorites album

Photos stored in the **Favorites** album are used to create the photo slideshow that you see on the Home screen. You can easily move photos from other albums to your Favorites album to create a visually pleasing display.

It's easy to add a photo to the Favorites album. While viewing the photo you would like to add, click Add to Album..., click the Favorites album, and then click OK.

My Albums

The **My Albums** folder contains all of the albums that you create on your computer. The albums on your computer will display with a **blue** binder.

Creating an album

To get started creating albums, click the My Albums folder and then click Create New Album. Enter a name and click OK. The album will appear in the **My Albums** folder. You can then begin adding photos to this new album.

Uploading Photos

Loading photos is easy! Simply attach a device or insert a card and follow the instructions below for copying/moving photos.

Attaching a USB Device

A USB device may be a camera, an external hard drive, or a USB stick. Attach the USB cable into your camera or external storage device. Then, plug the other end of the USB connector into one of the USB ports in the computer. To locate USB ports, refer to the **Quick Start Guide** that came with the computer.

Inserting a Camera Card

Insert your camera card into an SD to USB reader, and insert that into a USB port (see page 5).

After your device is plugged in, when the selection prompt appears, choose **Load Photos**. When the card appears on the 'From' side, the photos are ready to be copied or moved to your computer. For instructions on using the Photo Loader, click **Help**.

My Albums

My Albums contains all the albums you create on your computer. Here you can create new albums, edit existing albums or delete unwanted albums.

To view an album:
- **Click the Photos button**
- **Click the album group titled, My Albums**

Create an Album

Creating an album is quick and easy. To create a new album, click the Create New Album button, type in a name for the album, and then click Ok. Once you've created a new local album, you can begin moving or copying photos into it by uploading photos from your camera or external device or by moving photos from other albums.

Edit Album Information

Once you've created a new album, you can edit the album information. Simply click the Edit button at the bottom of the album, edit the fields you wish to change and click Save.

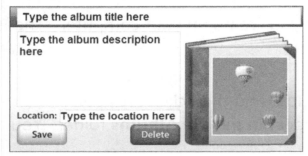

Viewing and Managing Photos

Viewing and managing the photos in your albums is simple and easy. You can switch the order of photos, choose a particular photo to be used as an album cover, move photos to other albums, print and much more!

To view and manage photos:
- **Click the Photos button**
- **Click the album group titled, My Albums**
- **Click an album**

Navigation Functions

Thumbnail View

Thumbnail view allows you to get a better idea of what, and how many, photos are in an album. It creates smaller representations of each photo so that you can easily find the photo you are looking for. Simply click the thumbnail of a photo to view it larger.

If you would like to change the order of the photos, click the **Organize** button that appears in the top right corner of the thumbnail view. Click a photo and use the arrow buttons to move the photo to the desired location. When you are happy with the order of the photos in the album, click Done.

Slideshow

Slideshow is a great way to show friends and family photos in your albums. Clicking the Slideshow button brings you to a picture viewer that will cycle through all the photos in the current album with a 10 second delay between each photo. Click **Next** to move to the next photo instead of waiting for the delay. Click **Previous** to get back to a photo you have passed. Clicking **Pause** will stop the slideshow. Once you are done viewing a slideshow, you can click Close to return to the last screen you were on.

Previous / Next

Use the ◀ and ▶ buttons to navigate through your photos. The ◀ button, located to the left of the current photo, will take you to the **previous** photo in the album. The ▶ button, located to the right of the current photo, will take you to the **next** photo in the album.

Photo Function Buttons

Share

Clicking the *Share* button will automatically attach the current photo to a blank email so that you can send it to friends and family.

Add to Album...

You can copy or move photos to any one of the local (blue) albums that you've created, including the **Favorites*** album. Simply use the Previous and Next buttons to find the photo that you would like copy or move and click Add to Album... Finally, choose a destination folder for the photo you are moving/copying.

* Photos added to your **Favorites** album appear on the **Home** screen.

Make Album Cover

The **Make Album Cover** option is only available for photos in your local (blue) albums. This feature allows you to select a photo to use as the album cover for the current album. While viewing a photo you want as the album cover, select **Make Album Cover**.

Delete

The Delete option is only available for photos in your local (blue) albums. It allows you to remove any unwanted photos or duplicates from the current album. While viewing a photo you want to delete, select **Delete**.

Edit Photo

The **Edit Photo** button is only available for photos in your local (blue) albums. While viewing a photo you want to edit, click Edit Photo. A variety of editing options will appear on the right for you to choose from. Select the editing option you would like to perform on the photo, and when you are happy with the newly edited photo, click Done.

TECH TIP: If you are just learning how to edit photos or are experimenting with the tools, you may want to create duplicates of the photos you are editing so you will not have to worry if you make a mistake. To do this, follow these instructions:

1. Go to **My Albums**.
2. Click **Create New Album** and name the album.
3. Go through your albums or your friends albums & find the photos you want to edit.
4. When you find a photo you would like to edit, Click Add to Album... and select the album you just created.
5. After you have finished looking for photos to edit, go to the album that you placed the photos in.
6. Start editing and have fun.
7. If you like how it looks when you have finished editing, you can add it to any album you would like or leave it in that album.

Rotate

This option allows you to rotate the photo using the following options:

- **Rotate Left** - Turns the photo 90 degrees counter-clockwise.
- **Rotate Right** - Turns the photo 90 degrees clockwise.
- **Flip Horizontal** - Flips the photo from Right to Left. For example, if the photo you were editing was ◀ and you click **Flip Horizontal,** then the photo would now be ▶ .
- **Flip Vertical** – Flips the photo top to bottom. If the photo you were editing was ▲ and you click **Flip Vertical,** then the photo would now be ▼ .
- **Free Rotate** - This button allows you to rotate your photo yourself. Clicking this button will put boxes in the four corners of your photo and a red dot at the center.

Click one of the boxes and, without lifting your finger, move the box in the direction you wish to turn the photo. Lift your finger when it is oriented to your liking.

- **Undo** - This button allows you to undo the last change made to your photo. There is no limit to the amount of times you can use this button.
- **Done** - When you are satisfied with your photo, clicking done will save all of your changes and take you back to the Edit Photo page. Do not click this button unless you are absolutely sure that you are satisfied with how your photo looks because you will not be able to undo the changes.

Crop

This option allows you to cut off sections of your photo. For instance, let's say that your family took a picture in front of a funny carnival background, but when you looked at the photo, you noticed that the area above the background is visible. With the crop tool, you can remove that section of the photo so that the area above the carnival background isn't visible.

Horizon

This option lets you rotate your photo so that line you set as the horizon will be perfectly horizontal.

Red Eye

This option allows you to remove certain amounts of the color red from either an entire picture or specific areas. The main use for this option is to remove the red eyes that occasionally show up in photos. The **Red-eye threshold** slider determines how much red is removed - slide this back and forth to get the effect you want. The **Choose eyes** button lets you focus the red-eye remover over specific areas. This is useful if the red removal seems to remove red from the wrong areas of the photo. Simply click the **Choose eyes** button and click the eyes in the photo. You can remove an area by clicking on it a second time. The **Search zone size** slider makes the eye zones smaller or larger.

Contrast

This option lets you adjust how your photo looks using a variety of options.

- **Brightness** - This slider will make your photo darker or brighter.
- **Contrast** - This slider will determine the difference between the light and dark colors in the photo. When the slider is moved to the right, the difference between the dark and light colors increase, but when the slider is moved left, the difference between the light and dark colors will decrease and become more similar.
- **Saturation** - This slider allows you to change the vibrancy of the colors in your photo. The more the slider is moved to the right, the more vivid the photo will be,

and the more the slider is moved to the left the more washed out the photo becomes.

- **Color Balance** - This slide allows you to adjust or change the color of the photo. This tool can be used to slightly modify a photo to your liking or to change the photo drastically to be artistic or zany.

Printing Photos

To print one or more photos in the current album, follow these instructions:

1. Click **Print**.
2. Click **Select Photos**.
3. Click the photo(s) you would like to print. You can click the photo(s) again to deselect.
4. Click Ok.
5. Click a printing option (see Printing Options below). The default printing option of "1 per page 8x10" will be selected. If this is what you want, simply click **Print**. To print several smaller copies of the photo on one page, click a different printing option, then click **Print**.

Printing Options

Sizes are shown in inches. The following sizes are available:

- 5 x 7 - will print one photo per page.
- 4 x 6 - will print two photos per page.
- 3 x 5 - will print four photos per page.
- 2.2 x 3.5 - will print photos six per page.
- 2.5 x 3 - will print eight photos per page.

NOTE: If you select an option that will print several photos per page, but you only choose one photo to print, only one photo will be printed in the smaller size.

Thumbnail View

This view allows you to see all of the photos in your current album. From this screen, you can see how many photos are in the album, view a specific photo, and organize your photos.

To view thumbnails

- **Click the Photos button**
- **Click the album group titled, My Albums**
- **Click an album**

Navigation

This view allows you to quickly navigate to a photo. Simply find the photo and click it to view that photo.

Organize

You can organize the photos in your albums and your friends' albums to your liking. To organize your albums, follow these instructions:

1. Click **Organize**, located in the top right corner.
2. Click the photo you want to move.
3. Use the arrow buttons, located in the top right corner, to move the photo to where you want it.
4. The ▲ and ▼ buttons moves the photo vertically by one row.
5. The ◀ and ▶ buttons move the photo horizontally by one column.
6. When you are satisfied with how the photos are arranged, click Done - located to the right of the arrow buttons.

Back to Photo View

This button will bring you back to photo view at the first photo in your album.

 # Calendar

This page lets you manage and print your calendar.

To use the calendar, click the Calendar button.

Managing Your Calendar

Add an Event

To add a new event to your calendar, perform the following steps:

1. Click the date of the event on the calendar. You can navigate through different months using the buttons at the top.
2. Click the **New Item** button. A popup window will appear.
3. Give the event a name.
4. Using the checkboxes, select what type of event you are creating. If it is a birthday or anniversary, the computer will remember these events each year, and you can skip ahead to step **9**. If it is an appointment or other type of event, continue to step **5**.
5. Click in the box to the right of the word **Location,** then type in a location for the event.
6. Enter a time for the event to start.
7. Select the duration of the event to indicate how long the event will last.

8. Click the **Reminder** droplist to set the reminder for the alarm. The **Reminder** is the amount of time before the event that you want the alarm to go off. Select **None** to set no alarm.

9. If it is a recurring event, click the **Frequency** droplist to select how often you would like the event to occur.

View Event Details

To view or change the details for an existing event on your calendar, follow these instructions:

1. Click the day of the event you would like to view. The event will appear in the **Daily Reminders** section.

2. Click the event in the **Daily Reminders** section. A pop-up window will appear displaying the settings and notes for that event.

3. At this point you may edit the information and click **Save** when you are done, or click **Cancel** to exit with no saved changes.

Edit an Event

To edit the details for an existing event on your calendar, follow these instructions:

1. Click the day of the event which needs to be edited. The event will appear in the **Daily Reminders** section.

2. Click the event in the **Daily Reminders** section. A pop-up window will appear with the settings for that event.

3. Make the appropriate changes and click **Save**.

Remove an Event

To remove an existing event on your calendar, follow these instructions:

1. Click the day of the event in the calendar. The event will appear in the **Daily Reminders** section.

2. Click the event in the **Daily Reminders** section. A pop-up window will appear with the settings for that event.

3. Click the **Delete** button. You will be asked to confirm the action.

Dismiss/Snooze a Reminder

When you set a reminder for an event and the reminder comes due, a window will open on your screen. You may either dismiss or snooze the reminder.

To dismiss a reminder, simply click the **Dismiss** button.

To snooze the reminder, click the **Snooze** button - this is like hitting the snooze button on an alarm clock. The reminder window will disappear and reappear again in about 5 minutes.

🖨 **Print - Click this button to print the calendar for the current month.**

Contacts/Address Book

Your contacts are stored in an Address Book that is similar to one you might keep at home. You can manage your contacts easily with the Address Book by storing addresses, phone numbers and other important information. You can also use your address book to easily email your contacts.

To use your Address Book and manage contacts, click the Contacts Button.

When you click the Contacts button, your Address Book is displayed. You will notice it looks very much like a real address book, complete with alphabetic tabs to allow you to organize and navigate through your list of contacts.

Alphabetic Tabs

Your contacts are stored in alphabetical order by last name. Use the alphabetic tabs to navigate through your contacts. For example, if the contact's last name is **"Smith"**, click the Q-S tab .

If you don't have a lot of contacts, you may see them all listed when you click alphabetic tabs that do not contain the first letter of a contact's last name. This is okay. The Address Book is designed to allow you to see all your contacts in this situation.

Left and Right Pages

Your electronic Address Book is organized a little differently than a traditional address book. You'll notice it has a left page and a right page. The left page is used to display a list of your contacts and the right page is used to display your contact's information. Once you begin adding contacts, you will see them listed in the left page. To display a contact's information, click the contact's name and you will see their details displayed in the right page. On the left page, you may notice some icons under some of your contacts' names.

Below is a list of icons and meanings.

- ✉ - This contact has an email address saved in your address book.

Contacts, Requests & Removed

The Address Book also displays three buttons at the top of the left page: Contacts, Requests and Removed. Clicking these buttons will change the function of the Address Book. The default function is Contacts to allow you to add, view, edit and remove contacts.

Managing Contacts

Add a Contact
1. Click **Add**

2. On the right page, enter the information for your new contact
3. Click **Save Contact** when you are done

View a Contact

1. Use the alphabetic tabs to navigate to the contact
2. Click the name of the contact
3. On the right page, you will see the contact's information

Edit a Contact

1. Use the alphabetic tabs to navigate to the contact
2. Click the contact's name to display their information on the right page
3. Make changes or additions to their info. The information is automatically saved once you enter it, unless the **Autosave contacts** option (see Settings) is unchecked.

Remove a Contact

You can permanently remove a contact. Once removed, the contact cannot be restored, so use with caution. To remove a contact, follow these instructions:

1. Use the alphabetic tabs to navigate to the contact
2. Click the contact's name to display their information on the right page
3. Click the **Delete** or **Remove** button. You will be asked to confirm the action

Add a Group

You can create email groups, which allow you to send a single email to multiple people without having to individually add each person into the **To:** field. To do so:

1. Click the **Add Group** button
2. On the right page, click in the **Group Name:** field, then type in the name of the group
3. Below the **Group Name:** field, you will see a list of your contacts. Select the contacts you wish to add to the group.
4. Click **Save Group button** when you are done

Edit a Group

1. Use the alphabetic tabs to navigate to the group you wish to change
2. Click the group's name to display its information on the right page
3. Make changes or additions to the name or members. The information is automatically saved once you enter it, unless the **Autosave contacts** option (see Settings) is unchecked.

Remove a Group

1. Use the alphabetic tabs to navigate to a group
2. Click the group's name to display its information on the right page
3. Click the **Delete** button. You will be asked to confirm the action.

Add/Change a Photo
1. Use the alphabetic tabs to navigate to the contact
2. Click the contact's name to display their information on the right page
3. Click the **Change Photo** button
4. A window will appear to allow you to browse through your local albums. Click the photo you would like to use and select the **OK** button.

Email a Contact

If you have entered an email address for a contact, you may click **Email** on the right page to address an email to them!

Duplicate Contacts

Check if contacts in your address book have the same info, Click Settings, then **Duplicates?** The **Merge Contacts** window will allow you to merge contact entries. Click on a pair and if there is conflicting information in the two entries (example: Contact 1 has the Home phone number as (555) 565-5459 and Contact 2 has the Home phone number as (557) 544-5085), you will be given a popup to let you choose what information you would like to keep.

 # Weather

This application allows you to view weather conditions for a specific zip code or city, as well as providing you with a 5 day forecast and a Doppler map.

If this is your first time using weather, enter your zip code in the box where it says Please enter your zip code here for your profile and then click the Save to Profile button. Once you have saved your zip code into your profile, whenever you click the Weather button, the weather for your zip code will automatically be displayed. To change your zip code:

1. Click the **Settings** button, located in the top right corner of the screen
2. Click the **General Settings** button, located in the top right corner of the screen
3. Click the **My Profile** button, located at the top of the column of buttons on the right
4. Change the zip code in the field labeled Zip
5. Click **Save Changes**
6. Click Close, which is the red button near the top right corner of the screen

To check weather for other cities, enter the zip code or name of the city in the white box to the left of the green **GO** button and then click **GO**. If there is more than one city with that name then select the one you want.

Click this button: to return to the weather for the zip code set in your profile.

Current Conditions

This section displays general information about current weather conditions for the selected zip code, including temperature in degrees Fahrenheit or Celsius (see below for details), humidity, wind, etc. and forecasts for day and evening.

Weather Map

The live Doppler radar map displays an animated view of the weather patterns for the selected zip code. If the location searched is outside the United States, the map will show a satellite view instead.

5 Day Forecast

At the bottom of your screen, you will see a 5-day forecast for the selected zip code. Click any day to display a more detailed forecast for that day in the **Current Conditions** section.

Changing Temperature Output

The temperatures are displayed in degrees Fahrenheit by default but you can change it to degrees Celsius by following these instructions:

1. If you are not already in the Weather application, click the **Weather** button; otherwise, skip to step 2.
2. Click the **Settings** button in the upper right-hand corner of the screen.
3. Select the temperature output that you would like your weather to be in (i.e. Fahrenheit or Celsius). A check mark will appear in the box next to the selected output.
4. After making your selection, click **Close**, which is located in the upper right-hand corner of the screen.

 # News

News allows you to view a list of updated headlines from various news sources available on the Internet. You must have a working internet connection to use the News application.

To read the news, click the News button.

Welcome to your electronic newspaper! When you click the **News** button, you will see a list of news headlines and a list of news category buttons along the right side of the headlines. Simply click a news headline to read the article. Click a category button to view headlines in that category - similar to browsing through different sections of the newspaper.

News Source

Your electronic newspaper allows you to change the source of the news. This is similar to choosing a different newspaper to read. The current news source is displayed at the top right corner of the list of headlines. Examples of news sources are Yahoo, CNN and ESPN. See the section below for changing the news source.

Change News Source/Category

To change the news source, follow these instructions:

1. Click **Change News Source**
2. Click the name of any news source.
3. Click **OK**.

You will see the headlines, news source and category buttons update to reflect your selection.

Change News Category

The category buttons are listed along the right side of the news headlines page. Click any category button to list the headlines for a particular category. For instance, if you clicked **Politics**, you will see the latest politics-related headlines from your selected news source.

Reading Articles

When you click a news headline to read the full story, the article will appear with function buttons across the top. When reading an article, you may use these buttons to add the article to your favorites, print it out, navigate or zoom in/out. When you are finished reading and want to view the headlines again, click the Back to News button to go back to the last page of headlines that you viewed.

Back to News

Click Back to News to return to the news headlines page.

◀ **Back** - Click Back to view the previous web page.

▶ **Forward** - Click Next to view the next web page.

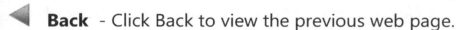 **Add to Favorites**

Click the Add to Favorites button to bookmark the site you are currently viewing. A pop-up window will appear so that you can edit the information for the bookmark. You can use the default name that appears in the Name field, or give your bookmark a unique name. You can also save the bookmark into an existing category using the category drop down menu, or create a new one in the "Or enter new" field.

Click Ok to add the bookmark, or Cancel to cancel adding the bookmark.

🖨 **Print - click this button to print the current page, or parts of the current article.**

 **Zoom In/Out** - Increase or decrease the size of the article.

 # Web

Use the Web application to view web sites with the built-in web browser.

To use the internet, click the Web button.

The Web application allows you to visit any web site on the Internet. You can also bookmark any site so that you can easily return to it at a later time. When you first enter the Web application, you will see the Quick Links page (see below). You can either click one of these sites to visit, or type in any other address in the address bar (see below.)

Web Toolbar Buttons

 Quick Links

Click this button to view the Quick Links page. This page displays some of the most useful and popular websites, grouped by category. Within each category are icons for the web sites that make up that category. You may need to move the slider down in order to see all of the categories.

To view one of the web sites, click the icon for that web site. For example, click **YAHOO!** to go to that website.

If you change your Home Page, clicking this button will take you to that page in place of the Quick Links page. To change your Home Page, follow these instructions:

1. Click *Web*.
2. Click *Settings*, located next to the *Help* button in the upper right-hand corner of your screen. This will bring up the *Browser Settings* page
3. Click the *Home Page:* text field.
4. Type the URL of the website you want to set as your new Home Page.

TECH TIP: If the website you want to set as your new Home Page is long or difficult to remember, then navigate to that page and use keyboard controls (instructions listed on Pages 19) to copy and paste the URL into this field.

TECH TIP: Using copy on a webpage is recommended over the use of the cut function because the cut function only works for text you typed yourself.

5. When you have either typed or pasted the URL into the text field, click the *Save*.
6. If you ever wish to change your Home Page back to the Quick Links page, click the *Use Quick Links* button on the *Browser Settings* page then click *Save*.

NOTE: Please be aware that if the website you set as your Home Page falls under a category that is blocked by the Web Filter then clicking this button will not take you to that page.

 Favorites

The Favorites button will take you to your list of bookmarked sites. These can also be organized into categories, which can be renamed at any time by clicking Edit, typing a new name and clicking Done. To navigate to a bookmarked website, click the Favorites button then click the name of the website that you've bookmarked. You can bookmark any website by clicking the Add to Favorites button (see below).

 Back

Click Back to view the previous web page.

 Forward

Click Forward after using the Back button to return to the next web page.

 Add to Favorites

Click the Add to Favorites button to bookmark the site you are currently viewing. A pop-up window will appear so that you can edit the information for the bookmark. You can use the default name that appears in the Name field or give your bookmark a unique name. You can also save the bookmark into an existing category using the category drop down menu or create a new one in the "Or enter new" field.

Click Ok to add the bookmark or Cancel to cancel adding the bookmark.

Address Bar

This is the address bar. Type the URL in here and click GO.	GO

The Address Bar is used to enter the URL, or address, of a website. To navigate to a specific web site, type the web site name, for example "www.yahoo.com" or "www.google.com", into the Address Bar and then click the GO button.

Additionally, the Address Bar can be used to search the Internet. Simply type in a company name or name of a person, place or thing into the Address Bar, then click GO to generate a list of search results for that word. In the search results list, click the blue underlined text to view a website that matches your search. When searching, you may enter a single word or combination of words into the Address Bar.

 Print

If you have a printer connected to your computer, click this button to print the current page, or parts of the current page (see **Print Request Settings** on page 116 for more info).

 **Zoom In/Out** - Increase or decrease the size of the web page.

Saving Pictures from the Web

To save pictures from the web, click the picture with your right mouse button. This will bring up a dialog box that says, "Do you want to save this image into an album?" Click the Ok button. You will then be given the option to select which album you wish to save the image in. When you have chosen the album you wish to put the image in, click Save, or if you wish to create a new album for it, click the New Album button, type the name of the album you wish to create, and click Ok. If at any time you change your mind about a decision, click Cancel

 # Games

For game functionality and rules:
- **Click the Games button**
- **Click the icon for the game that you would like instruction**
- **Click the Help button in the upper right corner of the screen**

 # More

This area lists additional applications available on your computer.

To view more applications available on your computer, click the More button.

 # Backup/Restore

Backup/Restore is a feature that allows you to easily backup your computer's information on an external hard disc - or on our server computers - for safekeeping. You may also easily restore your backed up information with this feature.

To use the Backup / Restore application:
- **Click the More button**
- **Click the Backup/Restore icon**

There are two ways to perform backups: locally or via the network. Network backup/restore is a paid service, where your files are stored on our server computers. It's easier to use, because backups will be done automatically - you don't need an external hard disc and only need to leave your computer on - and the backup will be run on a regularly scheduled basis. Local backups are done using your own external hard disc. You will need to manually perform the backups, but we'll help you set up reminders if you want!

Local Backup/Restore

Local Backups

There are three simple steps to performing a local backup:

1. Attach an external hard disc.
2. Run the backup.
3. Disconnect the hard disc.

These steps are described in the sections below.

Attach the Hard Disc

Simply plug in an external hard disc into one of the USB ports located on the back and/or side of your computer. The computer will automatically recognize that you have connected the hard disc, and will start to scan the hard disc to see how much space is available for backup use. Once the amount of space available has been determined, if there's enough for your backup, the Backup Now button will become enabled, and you can move to the next step.

Backup Data

Simply click the Backup Now button and your backup will begin. First, the computer will determine what files need to be backed up. You'll see a progress bar while this is happening. Next, the files will be saved to the attached hard disc. You will see another progress bar while the files are being backed up. When the progress bar disappears, your backup is finished!

Disconnect the Hard Disc

Once the progress bar has disappeared, unplug your hard disc, and put it in a safe place. Be sure you don't remove the hard disc until the progress bar has gone away, though.

Setting Backup Reminders

You can have your computer remind you to do backups on a regular basis. You can schedule these reminders to be once a week or once a month. On the **Backup/Restore** settings screen, simply click the check box next to the frequency of the reminder you want. When a reminder is set, it will appear in the **Notices** section of your **Home** screen. If you want to change the date that these reminders appear in your **Notices**, click

Calendar, click the day the reminder currently occurs, then click the reminder to open it for editing.

Restoring Data

If you ever need to restore backed up files onto your computer, follow these instructions:

1. Click **Backup/Restore**.
2. Attach your external backup disc.
3. Click **Restore Now** and your files will be copied back to your computer.

Network Backup/Restore

This is a paid service. You will need to purchase a backup subscription to use it. It is very convenient to use, and your data is stored for you on our servers.

Purchasing a Network Backup/Restore Subscription

To subscribe to our network backup service, simply click the Purchase Subscription button. This will take you to a popup page that allows you to securely purchase a backup subscription.

Network Backup

Once you have subscribed to our network backup service, your computer will automatically backup files to our servers - without you having to do anything! If you need to backup at a particular time, you can just click Network Backup Now, and your computer will start the backup process.

NOTE: ***You may only click the*** Network Backup Now ***button once in a 24 hour period.***

Network Restore

If you need to restore your data, please call support. The latest backup on our server will be copied to your computer. Once the restore has completed, you will be asked to restart your computer.

CD Player

This application allows you to listen to CDs with an external drive you supply. You can have your CD play in the background while you use the computer's other functions.

To use the CD application:

- **Click the More button**
- **Click the CD Player icon**

Album Art

If you are connected to the internet, and the information is found, the album art for your CD will appear in the box in the top left corner. Otherwise a default picture and the words "no album art found" will appear in the box in the top left corner.

Track List

This is a list of all audio tracks on your CD and the length of each track. Again, if you are connected to the internet, and track info is found, the list will show the track titles; otherwise the title will appear as the track number. The track list not only shows you what tracks are on your CD but also lets you select a specific track to play. To choose a track you want to play, click the title of the track. The icon to the left of the track title shows its current play status.

▶ Indicates that the current track is not playing

♫ Indicates that the current track is playing

Now Playing

Located just beneath the Track List is the Now Playing info panel. This shows you what track is currently playing, how long the track is, and how far into the track you are. If Shuffle and/or Repeat are activated then it will be displayed in this panel to the right of current track title.

Artist: / Album:

Located beneath the **Album Art** are the Artist and Album information. If you are connected to the internet, these will show the name of the artist & album that you are currently playing.

To insert a CD, press the small button on the CD tray, or, if you are in the **CD Player** application, click **Eject CD**. When the tray pops open, place your CD in the tray, pressing firmly around the center until you hear or feel it snap on. Then gently press the tray in toward the computer to close. You will hear a click when the tray is closed. It should close easily and require only gentle pressure. Never force a disc into the tray.

NOTE: Before pressing the tray in, ensure the disc is mounted firmly on the tray. If the disc is loose or falling off the tray, then it is not mounted properly and you run the risk of damaging the tray and possibly the drive.

Playing a CD

Playing a CD is easy! Simply insert a CD into an external Optical disk drive (connected via a USB 3.0 port, see page 5) and you will be prompted to play the CD. If you are in the CD Player application, just click the play button. CD function buttons are described below.

CD Player Function Buttons

Located beneath the Now Playing info panel are several buttons. These buttons are used to control the playing of the CD.

▷	**Play**	The Play button serves two purposes. If you have a CD in your disk drive and the CD player is not currently running, pressing Play will start the application. If a track is paused, clicking Play will resume play.
❚❚	**Pause**	If a track is currently playing, the Play button will change to a Pause button. Clicking Pause will pause the track at whatever point in the track you are, clicking Play will continue the track from that point.
▣	**Stop**	The Stop button turns off the CD Player.
◀◀	**Previous Track / Replay**	This button allows you to go to the track that is listed directly before the current track on the Track List; however if the current track is the first track, clicking this button will bring you to the last track on the Track List. If you are more than 5 seconds into the current track, then clicking this button will restart the current track.
▶▶❙	**Next Track**	This button allows you to go to the track that is listed directly after the current track on the Track List; however if the current track is the last track, then clicking this button will bring you to the first on the Track List
	Shuffle	Clicking Shuffle activates Shuffle mode. When Shuffle mode is activated, the tracks will play in a random order; however the Previous Track button will play the track played before the current track.
	Repeat	Repeat allows you to choose what happens when a track finishes playing.

- Clicking Repeat once will set it so that track restarts when it finishes playing. The display will read, "Repeat One".
- Clicking Repeat twice will set it so that it plays the next track on the list, but after the last track finishes playing, it will replay all of the tracks. The display will read, "Repeat All".
- Clicking Repeat three times will turn off the Repeat feature. The display will be blank.
- If Repeat is not on, then the CD Player will turn off when the last track finishes playing.

	Eject	Clicking Eject will open the disk drive.
	Back	Located in the top right corner, the Back button will take you back to the More main page; however if you do not click Stop before clicking Back the CD Player will continue to play.

Calculator

Use the calculator to perform basic math calculations. When you click the equals button (=), a running tab will be displayed to the right. Below is a list of functions.

Calculator Functions

Bksp	Delete one number at a time.
%	Determines a percentage. For example, 8% is .08 and is displayed as "8%".
1/x	Divides one by the number entered. For example, 5 then 1/x = 0.2
+/-	Change the number from positive to negative.
.	Adds a decimal point.
C	Clear - Clears the current line or entry.
AC	All Clear - Clears everything. All the past functions as well as the current line.
/	Divides two numbers. For example, 8 / 4 = 2
X	Multiplies two numbers. For example, 3 x 3 = 9
-	Subtracts two numbers. For example, 4 - 2 = 2
+	Adds two numbers. For example, 3 + 4 = 7
=	Determines the result of the current operation.

Alternate Input Method

Besides using the buttons on the screen, you can also use your keyboard to enter numbers and functions.

Conversion

This page allows you to convert measurements, weights, and distances between different units.

Converting Between Units

To convert between different units, perform the following steps:

1. Enter the measurement, weight, or distance that you would like to convert from.
2. Use the drop down menu ▼ to select the units you are converting from.
3. Use the drop down menu ▼ to select the units you would like to convert to.
4. Click the Go button.

NOTE: The conversion will be measured out to two decimal places.

DVD Player

This is your computer's DVD player. You can watch videos that you insert into an external DVD/CD drive supplied by you.

To use the DVD Player:

- **Click the More button**
- **Click the DVD Player icon**

Inserting a DVD

To insert a DVD, press the small button on the DVD tray door, or, if you are in the DVD Player application, click "Please insert a DVD". When the tray pops open, place your DVD in the tray. Then gently press the tray in to close. You will hear a click when the tray is closed. It should close easily and require only gentle pressure. Never force a disc into the tray.

NOTE: Before pressing the tray in, ensure the disc is mounted firmly on the tray. If the disc is loose or falling off the tray, then it is not mounted properly and you run the risk of damaging the tray and possibly the drive.

Watching a DVD

Watching a DVD is easy! Simply insert a DVD into the computer and you will be prompted to play the movie. If you are in the DVD Player application, just click Play Movie.

Ejecting a DVD

To eject a DVD that is in the DVD tray, click Open DVD Tray.

DVD Player Toolbar

Once you have inserted a DVD and clicked Play Movie, the movie will begin to play and you will see the DVD toolbar appear at the bottom of the screen. Use this toolbar to access DVD functions and to control the playback of the DVD. The following functions are available from your DVD toolbar:

Menu

If the DVD has menu options, click the Menu button to display a list of the available options for the video. Menu options may include chapter and scene selection, subtitles and bonus features.

▷	**Play**	Click to start or continue playing the DVD. It will then change to the Pause button.
❚❚	**Pause**	Click to Pause the DVD at the current position. It will then change to the Play Button.
▢	**Stop**	Click the Stop button to stop the video and exit. To play, select Play Video.
▷▷	**Fast Forward**	Click the Fast Forward button to fast forward the video. The video will continue to fast forward until you click the Play button.
◁◁	**Rewind**	Click the Rewind button to rewind the video. The video will continue to rewind until you click the Play button.
▷▷❘	**Next Chapter**	Click the Next Chapter button to skip ahead to the next chapter.
❘◁◁	**Previous Chapter**	Click the Previous Chapter button to skip back to the previous chapter.
◯	**Volume**	Drag the volume slider left or right to lower or raise the volume.

Subtitles

If the video has subtitles, select the Subtitles button to toggle the subtitles on or off.

File Manager

The File Manager allows you to manage the files and folders on your computer. You may move files, delete files and create new folders.

To use the File Manager:

- **Click the More button**
- **Click the File Manager icon**

Files & Folders

There are many types of files: documents, images, PDFs, etc. For example, the Write application is used to create documents and you may get image attachments in email. The File Manager is used to move, copy, and delete files.

Your computer uses folders as a way to organize your files. For example, you may create a "Taxes" folder to store documents that are related to your taxes. The File Manager is used to move, delete or create new folders.

Source & Destination panels

The File Manager has two panels: **From** and **To**. The files and folders on your computer are displayed in these panels.

The **From** panel is used to select files/folders to be moved, copied, or deleted. The **To** panel is where you will select a destination folder for moved or copied files.

Using the File Manager

Create a Folder

Click the **New Folder** button to create a new folder in the **To** panel. Enter a name & click **OK**.

Select a File/Folder

To select a file or folder, simply click the check box: ☑ to the left of file's or folder's name. If you wish to select all of the files in the current folder, click the topmost checkbox.

Rename a File/Folder

To rename a file or folder, simply select a file or folder, then click Rename. A dialog box will appear to allow you to type a new name for your file or folder. If you are satisfied with the new name clicking Ok will save the change; however if you wish to keep the name the same, clicking Cancel will restore the original name.

Delete a File/Folder

In the **From** panel, select the file(s) or folder(s) you want to delete, and then click the **Delete** button. You will be asked to confirm the delete.

NOTE: When a folder is deleted, all the contents of that folder will be deleted. Please use delete with caution.

Move a File/Folder

When you want to move a file or folder, follow these instructions:

1. Find the file/folder you want to move in the **From** panel and select it.
2. Find the destination folder in the **To** panel and click it.
3. Click **Move**.

Copy a File/Folder

When you want to move a file or folder, follow the instructions:

1. Find the file/folder you want to copy in the **From** panel and select it.
2. Find the destination folder in the **To** panel and click it.
3. Click **Copy**

Open a Folder

To open a folder, click the folder name.

Open a File

To open a file, click the file name then click **Open**, located to the right of the active folder's name. The file will then open in the appropriate application.

If the file you are opening is an audio or video file, then the media player will appear in a popup, so that you will be able to listen to or view that file.

Back button

If you have opened a folder and want to return to the previous folder, click the button, located to the left of the current folder name.

Major Folders   *(NOTE: These folders cannot be deleted)*

Documents

This folder is the default location for saving text-based files. These include, but are not limited to: Write/Word documents, slideshows, and PDFs

Photos

This folder is the default location for saving picture files. This folder also contains all your locally saved photo albums. Clicking on an album's folder will allow you to see thumbnails of the pictures in that album's folder. You can also select pictures in order to Copy or Move them to a different folder. If you **Rename** an album's folder, it will also rename the corresponding album, with the exception of the Favorites album.

USB

This folder will only appear if you have an external hard drive or USB flash drive, also referred to as a thumb drive or memory stick, or a camera memory card, plugged into your computer. Clicking on this folder will show you all the files that are saved on the

USB device. You will be able to Copy and Move files from the device to your computer and vice versa.

Data Disc

This folder will only appear if you have a disc, with the exception of a music CD or a video DVD, in the disk drive. Clicking on this folder will show you all the files that are saved on the Disc, and you will be able to Copy files to your computer. When this folder is selected but not open an **Eject** button will appear next to the **Open** button. Clicking this will open the disc tray so that you may remove the disc from your computer.

 # Kindle Reader

The Kindle Reader application will allow you to read eBooks (electronic books) and listen to audio books on your computer that you purchase from Amazon.com! This will require you to have - or create - an Amazon.com account. Amazon.com is the largest bookseller on the internet. Opening an account with Amazon.com is free, but you will need to purchase the eBooks to read them on your computer. If you have a Kindle device, any books you purchase on Amazon.com can be read on both your Kindle and your computer.

Getting Started

To use the Kindle Reader, you will need an email address to create an.com account. If you do not have an email address, please create one and then return.

When you first open the Kindle Reader application, you will be presented with the "Sign In" screen.

Create an Account

If you do not have an account, you may create one now.

1. Enter your email address in the email of the Sign In screen
2. Click the circle next to "I am a new customer"
3. Click the button labeled, "Sign In using our secure server"
4. Enter your name, your email address again, and a password (twice)
5. Click "Create account"

You will be able to access the Kindle Reader now.

Sign In

If you have an Amazon.com account, you can sign in now. Enter your email address and password into the fields  of the Sign In screen, and then click the button labeled, "Sign In using our secure server". You may need to click the "Get Started Now" button.

You will be able to access the Kindle Reader now.

Kindle Library

When you sign into your Amazon.com account, you will be presented with your library. If you have purchased books or have borrowed books from the Library (requires a Library card and PIN from your preferred branch), you will see them here. Simply click a book to begin reading it!

Library Toolbar

The library toolbar contains icons for tools you can click to manage your library of books.

Sync

Click this button to synchronize the Kindle Reader with your Kindle device.

Settings

Click this button to get Help or Sign Out.

Search

Click this button to search through your library for a particular book. You may search by author or book title.

Kindle Store

Click the "Kindle Store" button to go to the Amazon.com website. This is where you may purchase new eBooks to read on your computer. Click the "Reader" button at the top of the screen to get back to your reader at any time.

Local Library

Some local libraries will allow you to borrow e-books on-line for a set period of time. You can then read or listen to these e-books on your computer or download them to your Kindle device. To find out how to borrow books from your library follow these instructions:

1. Call or visit your local library to find out if they offer e-books.
2. Confirm that you have a library account (card and PIN number) with that library.
3. Go to your local library website and locate the eBooks section (some libraries may call this Digital Downloads, Download Books, Digital Content or OverDrive). If you

are having difficulty finding this section, it is recommended that you ask a librarian for help or call your library and ask for instructions.

4. Search for and check out your Kindle book selections. When prompted, log in with your library card ID (and PIN, if required). If you need to request a hold on a title, use your personal e-mail address to make the hold.

5. Once you've checked out your title, choose Get for Kindle. You'll be redirected to Amazon.com's Public Library Loan page for that title. (You may be required to log in to your Amazon.com account -- or create a new account -- if you're not already logged in). Choose your device from the **Deliver to** menu, and choose Get library book to send the book to your reading app or device.

Reading Books

Overview

Once you are reading a book, simply click the arrows to the left or right of the text to turn the page backwards or forwards. The progress bar at the bottom of the screen shows you how far into the book you are.

Book Toolbar

The book toolbar contains icons for tools you can use while you are reading one of your books.

Library

Library Click this button to return to your library of books.

Show/Hide Toolbar

Click this button to show or hide the book toolbar.

Navigate

Click this button for navigation options. You will be able to navigate to the following locations in the book:

- Cover
- Table of Contents
- Beginning
- Location... (a specific page)
- Book Extras (additional information about the book and/or author)

Format / Text Size

Click this button to access formatting options for the reader. You will be able to change the following options:

- Font Size (size of the letters)
- Margins
- Color Mode (black text on white background -OR- brown text on sepia background -OR- white text on black background)

Click "Apply Settings" to confirm your changes, or click "Cancel" to ignore changes.

Bookmark

 Click this button to add a bookmark. A bookmark will be added to the page:

Click any bookmark to remove it.

To see all your bookmarks, click the "Note" button in the toolbar (see below).

Note

Click this button to highlight text or to manage and go to your notes and bookmarks.

To create a note, click a word, or drag to select words, and then click "Note". This will open a window for you to type in a note. Click "Save" to save the note. Click "Cancel" to back out of the operation.

To highlight text, click a word, or drag to select words, and then click "Highlight".

To go to a bookmark or note, click the Note button on the toolbar, then click a bookmark or note.

Media Player

The Media Player lets you play and enjoy audio and video files that you have saved on your computer. You can watch videos or listen to music, using this application, or have music playing in the background while you enjoy the other features your computer has to offer.

Making a Playlist

A playlist is a user-created list of media files, and lets you listen or watch these files without having to search through all of your files. The buttons below the **Pick the playlist** selection window can be used to create, rename, or delete playlist(s). The buttons are:

Add

Use this button to create a playlist. After clicking this button, a popup will appear asking you to "Enter the name of the new playlist". Type a name for your playlist, then click the green *OK* button. You can use the *Add* button to create as many playlists as you want.

Rename

Use this button to change the name of a playlist. Select the playlist you wish to rename from the **Pick the playlist** selection window; then click the *Rename* button. After clicking this button, a popup will appear asking you to "Enter the new name of the playlist". Type a name for your playlist, then click the green *OK* button.

Remove

Use this button to delete a playlist. Select the playlist you wish to rename from the **Pick the playlist** selection window; then click the *Remove* button.

Managing a Playlist

After creating a playlist, you can then fill it with your audio and video files so that you can play them. The buttons at the top of the playlist are:

Add Media

Use this button to add music and videos to a playlist. To do this, follow these instructions:

1. Click *More*.
2. Click *Media Player*.
3. Select a playlist from the **Pick a playlist** selection window.
4. Click the *Add Media* button.
5. After clicking Add Media, an **Open File** popup will appear. Select the file(s) you want by click the check box next to the file's name.

6. After you choose the file(s) to add to your playlist, click the green **Open** button. Tech Tip: Only files in the Multimedia folder can be added to a playlist. If you have media files in saved in other folders that you would like in your playlist, go to the **File Manager** and move them to the Multimedia folder.

Remove Media

Use this button to remove music or videos from a playlist. Select the song or video you wish to remove from your playlist; then click the **Remove Media** button. This will remove the file from your playlist, but you can add it back at any time using the **Add Media** button.

Move Up / Move Down

Use these buttons to change the order in which your songs are played. **Move Up** moves the selected file towards the top of the list, and **Move Down** moves the selected file towards the bottom of the list.

Enjoying your Media

When you want to enjoy music or a video, select a playlist to play from or select the **All** playlist, which contains all of your media files. The buttons used to play your music and videos are:

▷ Play

Clicking the **Play** button will start a song or video that has been selected from the current playlist or continue the song or video that is currently paused. If there is no song or video selected, the first item in the playlist will start. Click the **Full Screen** button (below viewer) to expand the display, click **Close** to return to the smaller image.

❚❚ Pause

If there is already a song or video playing, the **Play** button will switch to a **Pause** button. Clicking the **Pause** button will pause the current song or video.

■ Stop

This button ends the current song or video. If a song or video is stopped, pressing the play button will start it from the beginning.

Previous / Replay

This button switches from the song or video that is currently playing to the one that comes directly before it in the playlist; if the current song or video is the first item in the playlist, clicking this button will bring you to the last song or video in the playlist. If you are more than 5 seconds into the current song or video, then clicking this button will restart the current song or video, instead of starting the previous song or video.

 **Next**

This button switches from the song or video that is currently playing to the one that comes directly after it in the playlist; however if the current track is the last song or video in the playlist, then clicking this button will bring you to the first item in the playlist.

Shuffle

Clicking Shuffle activates Shuffle mode. When Shuffle mode is activated, the songs and/or videos will play in a random order. The **Next** button will skip to a random song or video, however the **Previous** button will play the song or video played before the current track.

Repeat

Repeat allows you to choose what happens when a song or video finishes playing.

- Clicking **Repeat** once will repeat the current song or video, "Repeat One".
- Clicking **Repeat** twice will set it so that it plays the next song or video on the list, but after the last track finishes playing, it will replay all of the tracks, "Repeat All".
- Clicking **Repeat** three times will turn off the Repeat feature. The display will be blank.
- If **Repeat** is not on, then the Media Player will turn off when the last song or video finishes playing.

Video Viewing Window

Located below the **Pick a playlist** selection window is the **Video Viewing Window**. This is where any video file you wish to view will play.

Eject CD

If there is a CD in your disc drive, clicking this button will open the disc drive.

Back

Located in the top right corner, the **Back** button will take you back to the **More** main page. If you do not click **Stop** before clicking **Back,** the Media Player will continue to play.

Rotate

When playing certain types of video files, a **Rotate** button will appear below the **Video Viewing Window**. Clicking this button lets you rotate the video 90 degrees to the left; however the rotation will not take effect until the next time you play the video.

Supported File Formats

Below is a list of common audio and video file formats that are known to be supported by your computer. Be aware that there may be other formats that will work with your computer but these formats are guaranteed.

Audio Formats supported

.aac	.aif	application/x-mplayer2	audio/annodex	audio/mpeg
audio/ogg	audio/wav	audio/x-ms-wma	audio/x-ogg	audio/x-wav
.axa	.m4a	.mp3	.oga	.wav
.wma				

Video Formats supported

.3gp	.anx	application/annodex	application/asx	application/ogg
application/x-ms-wmp	application/x-ms-wms	application/x-nsv-vp3-mp3	application/x-ogg	.asf
.avi	.axv	.divx	.flv	.m2v
.m4v	.mov	.mp4	.mpe	.mpeg
.mpg	.ogg	.ogv	video/annodex	video/divx
video/flv	video/mp4	video/mpeg	video/ogg	video/quicktime
video/webm	video/x-m4v	video/x-ms-asf	video/x-ms-asf-plugin	video/msvideo
video/x-ms-wm	video/x-ms-wmp	video/x-wmv	video/x-ms-wvx	video/x-ogg
video/x-wmv	.webm	.wmp	.wmv	

PDF Viewer

This application allows you to view PDF files.

To use the PDF Viewer:

- **Click the More button**
- **Click the PDF Viewer icon**

A PDF file is a type of document. PDF stands for "Portable Document Format". PDF files are commonly used on the Internet to display information. Examples of PDF files are IRS tax forms, bank statements, instruction manuals and articles.

PDF files can be viewed on the Internet or downloaded to your computer for later viewing. This application allows you to view PDF files on the Internet and also download them to your computer.

PDF Viewer Functions

Open	Click Open to select the PDF file you would like to view. The File Browser will open, displaying the files/folders in your computer. If you have downloaded a PDF from an email sent to you, or from the Internet, you will find that PDF in your "Documents" folder. Select the PDF you would like to open, and

then click Open in the File Browser.

Close   When you are finished with viewing a PDF file, click Close, and the PDF file will close.

Save As   If you want save a copy of the PDF file you are viewing, click Save As. The File Browser will open, displaying the files in your computer. You may select a new destination and name for the file. Click Save in the File Browser when you are done.

Previous Page   Click this button to go to the previous page in the PDF file.

Next Page   Click this button to go to the next page in the PDF file.

Zoom In   Click this button to magnify the size of the display in the PDF file.

Zoom Out   Click this button to reduce the size of the display in the PDF file.

Rotate Right Click this button to rotate the displayed PDF file to the right.

Rotate Left   Click this button to rotate the displayed PDF file to the left.

Print   Click this button to print from the current file, (see **Print Request Settings** on page 116 for more info).

Photo Loader

The Photo Loader allows you to import photos from your media to your computer. You may create new Albums and import photos into them.

To use the Photo Loader application:

- **Click the More button**
- **Click the Photo Loader icon**

Files & Folders

There are many types of files: documents, images, PDFs, etc. The Photo loader will only show images and folders. There may be other documents on the media but they will be hidden so you can easily select photos and put them into the albums.

Source & Destination panels

The File Manager has two panels: **From** and **To**. The files and folders on your computer are displayed in these panels.

The **From** panel is used to select files/folders to be moved, copied, or deleted. It shows you all the removable media that you have attached to the computer. You can have memory sticks, data CDs or memory cards. The **To** panel is where you will select a destination folder for moved or copied files. It shows you all the local photo albums you have already created. You can create new ones or select existing ones in this panel.

Using the File Manager

Note: Some actions are not available depending on the media that is being imported. For instance you cannot create, rename or delete files or folders on CDs or locked media.

Create a Folder

Click the **New Folder** button to create a new folder in the **To** panel. Enter a name & click **OK**.

Select a File/Folder

To select a file or folder, simply click the check box: ☑ to the left of file's or folder's name. If you wish to select all of the files in the current folder, click the topmost checkbox.

Rename a File/Folder

To rename a file or folder, simply select a file or folder, then click **Rename**. A dialog box will appear to allow you to type a new name for your file or folder. If you are satisfied with the new name clicking **Ok** will save the change; however if you wish to keep the name the same, clicking **Cancel** will restore the original name.

Delete a File/Folder

In the **From** panel, select the file(s) or folder(s) you want to delete, and then click the **Delete** button. You will be asked to confirm the delete.

Note: When a folder is deleted, all the contents of that folder will be deleted. Please use delete with caution.

Move a File/Folder

1. When you want to move a file or folder, follow these instructions:
2. Find the file/folder you want to move in the **From** panel and select it.
3. Find the destination folder in the **To** panel and click it.
4. Click **Move**.

Copy a File/Folder

1. When you want to move a file or folder, follow the instructions:
2. Find the file/folder you want to copy in the **From** panel and select it.
3. Find the destination folder in the **To** panel and click it.
4. Click Copy

Open a Folder

To open a folder, click the folder name.

Open a File

To open a file, click the file name then click **Open**, located to the right of the active folder's name. The file will then open in the photo viewer.

If the file you are opening is an audio or video file, then the media player will appear in a popup, so that you will be able to listen to or view that file.

Back button

If you have opened a folder and want to return to the previous folder, click the button, located to the left of the current folder name.

 # Scanner

The Scanner application allows you to use your HP scanning printer to scan, copy, and save physical documents and photos as digital files, **simply pressing the Scan button on the HP All-in-One Printer will not scan items into your computer**.

To use the Scanner application:

- **Click the More button**
- **Click the Scanner icon**

Scanning Options

The *Scanner* application offers you two varieties of scanning described below.

Scan a Document

This option allows you to scan a document and save it as PDF file. To do so follow these instructions:

1. Click *More*.
2. Click *Scanner*.
3. Click the *Scan a Document* button. Your screen will change to the scanner setup page.
4. Place the document you wish to scan face down on your scanner, while making sure that the document is against the front and right corners of the glass.
5. Click the *Scan* button on your screen, which will start the scanning process.
6. When your scan is complete, the completed scan page will appear with the result of the scan. You can save this scan as a PDF file by clicking the *Save Document* button or discard the document by clicking *Cancel*.
7. After clicking the Save This Scan button, a **Save File** popup will appear. Click the white box next to the word **Name**; then type a name for your file.
8. You can then choose a folder to place your file in or leave it in the documents folder, which is selected by default.
9. When you have selected a folder, click the green *Save* button. However, if you change your mind about wanting to save this file, click the red *Cancel* button.

Scan a Photo

This option allows you to scan a photo, allowing you more control over the end result, and then add it to one of your albums. To do so follow these options:

1. Click More.

2. Click Scanner.
3. Click the Scan a Photo button. Your screen will change to the scanner setup page.
4. Place the photo you wish to scan face down on your scanner, while making sure that the photo is against the front and right corners of the glass.
5. Click the Preview Scan on your screen, which will start the scanning process.
6. When the scanning process finishes, you will be given a Scan Preview which lets you adjust several aspects:
    o **Rotate** lets you rotate the photo 90 degrees to the **Right** or **Left**.
    o **Crop** allows you to choose the exact area of the photo you are scanning, eliminating empty borders. the several cropping options that are available to you are:
        - None, which means no cropping will be done.
        - 3.5x 5
        - 4 x 6
        - 5 x 7
        - 8 x 10
        - Free, this allows you to arbitrarily adjust the size of the cropping area using the gray squares, located at the corners and edges of the area.
    (Tech Tip: You can move the cropping area by clicking inside it and dragging it to the area of your choice.)
    o **Portrait** and **Landscape** are used to adjust the fixed crop sizes. For example, if you select 3.5 x 5 with portrait selected, the crop area will be 3.5 inches wide and 5 inches tall. If you select 3.5 x 5 with landscape selected, the crop area will be 5 inches wide and 3.5 inches tall.
7. When you have finished fine-tuning your scan, click Final Scan, which will rescan your photo with your adjustments.
8. When the scan is complete, click the Save Photo button. If you do not wish to save your scan, click the Cancel button.
9. After clicking the Save button, your photo albums will appear in a popup. Choose an album to place the photo in, then click Save.
10.   After choosing an album, you should name your photo. A popup will appear asking you to "Enter a name for this photo:", click on the white box and type a name for your photo.
11.   When you have finished typing a name for your photo, click the OK button.

Slideshow Viewer

This application allows you to view slideshow files (.ppt, .pptx, and .odp) that you have saved on your computer or that have been emailed to you as an attachment.

To use the Slideshow Viewer application:

- **Click the More button**
- **Click the Slideshow Viewer icon**

Slideshow Navigation Buttons

Open	This button lets you view a previously saved slideshow.	
Close	This button lets you close the slideshow.	
Previous	This button allows you to go to the previous slide in the slideshow	
Next	This button allows you to go to the next slide in the slideshow.	
Back	Located in the top right corner, the Back button will return you to the More main page.	

Spreadsheets

This application allows you to view, edit, and create spreadsheet files. These files are saved in the ".xls" format and are compatible with Microsoft Excel. When you first start up the application, a new file with three blank sheets will be opened.

The following instructions assume that you have:

- **Click the More button**
- **Click the Spreadsheets icon**

Terms to know

Here is a list of terms and techniques used in this guide that are vital to know:

- Cell - Sheets are divided into columns (represented by letters) and rows (represented by numbers). Cells are the space formed by the overlapping of columns and rows, and are referred to by the column and row. For example a cell that is in the 4th column and 6th row is Cell D6. Cells can contain text, numbers, or functions.

- Highlight - To highlight cells, click and hold the left mouse button on a cell then move the cursor until all the cells you want to highlight are purple.

- Drag - You can move cells by dragging them to a new location. To do this highlight the cell or cells you want to move, then click and hold the left mouse button on the cells. Finally, move the cursor and the outline of the cells to the new location.

Spreadsheets Functions

Button	Function	Description
New	**Create a New File**	Click New to create a new, blank spreadsheet. When you first open the Spreadsheets application, a new, blank document is created for you.
Open	**Open Existing File**	Click Open to open an existing spreadsheet. The File Browser window appears to help you find a spreadsheet to open. If the spreadsheet you want to open is in a folder, click the folder name to open the folder and list its contents. Once you find the spreadsheet you want to open, click the name of the spreadsheet and then click Open.
Save	**Save Spreadsheet**	Click Save to save the current spreadsheet. The File Browser window appears the first time you save a file to help you find a place to store the new spreadsheet. It's a good idea to save your spreadsheet periodically - even if you are not finished.
Save As	**Save Spreadsheet As another Name**	Click Save As to save the current spreadsheet under a new name. The File Browser window appears the first time you save a file to help you find a place to store the new spreadsheet. It's a good idea to save your spreadsheet periodically - even if you are not finished.
Close	**Close Spreadsheet**	Closes sheet, you will be asked if you wish to save first.
(printer icon)	**Print Spreadsheet**	Click to print the current spreadsheet. You'll need to have a printer turned on and connected to your computer (see page 116). For more help with printers, click Settings, Printer Settings, then click Help.
Back	**Go Back to More**	Click Back to close the Spreadsheet application and go back to the More page of applications.

 **Select a Sheet**

When creating a spreadsheet file, you start with three blank sheets - Sheet1, Sheet2, and Sheet3. You can switch between these sheets by using the **Sheet Selection** drop down menu, located on the left-hand side of the very top row. Click the button and select the sheet you wish to switch to.

When saving files, folders can be used to help organize your files. The New Folder button in the file browser allows you to create a new folder. To create a new folder, click New Folder, type a name for your folder, click Ok and you'll see your new folder. To store a file in that folder, click the folder name, click Open to open the folder, then then click Save to save the file in that folder.

Deleting a Spreadsheet

To Delete a spreadsheet, open **File Manager**, see page 72, then using the left pane , locate the file you wish to delete, select the file, then click **Delete**.

Toolbar Buttons

At the top of the Spreadsheets application is a toolbar with buttons that provide helpful functions. Click the buttons in the toolbar to create different text effects or format your document. It's fun to experiment so be creative! Don't worry about remembering them all though because, if you forget what a button does, you can bring up a **Tool Tip** by placing the mouse cursor on top of the button. Below is a list of toolbar buttons.

 Font Type

Drop down menu to display a list of font types. Select the font you like, and the text you type will be in that font.

Font Size

Drop down menu to display a list of font sizes. Select a size you like, and the text you type will be in that size.

 Font Color

Click the **Font Color** button to display a list of font colors. Select a color you like, and the text you type will be in that color.

Cell Color

Click the **Cell Color** button to display a list of cell colors. Select a color that you like, and the cell will appear in that color.

 Bold

Creates **bold text**.

 Italic

Creates italic text.

 Underline

Creates underlined text.

 Horizontal Alignment

Dropdown to select horizontal alignment. See options below.

☰	**Align Left**	Creates text aligned with the left margin of the cell.
☰	**Align Center**	Creates text that is centered between the side margins of the cell.
☰	**Align Right**	Creates text that is aligned with the right margin of the cell.
☰	**Justified**	Fills gaps between the words so that the text fits evenly between the margins. Similar to a newspaper column.
▼	**Vertical Alignment**	Drop down to select the vertical alignment of the cell. See options below.
	Top	Creates text aligned with the upper margin of the cell.
	Center	Creates text that is centered between the top and bottom margins of the cell.
	Bottom	Creates text aligned with the lower margin of the cell. Default.
General ▼	**Number Format**	Drop Down to select the format of numbers. See options below.
	General	This format leaves the number exactly the same as it is entered.
	1,234.00	This format gives displays two decimal places and inserts commas where needed.
	1,234	This format rounds up to the nearest whole number and inserts commas where needed.
	$1,234.00	This format displays the value in the form of US currency and inserts commas where needed.
	$1,234	This format displays the value rounded up to the nearest US dollar and inserts commas where needed
	1,234.00%	This format displays the value as a percent with two decimal places and inserts commas where needed
	1,234%	This format displays the value as a percent rounded to the nearest whole number. and inserts commas where needed
	DD/MM/YY	This format displays the value as a date in the form of day/month/year.
	MM/DD/YY	This format displays the value as a date in the form of month/day/year.

Borders		Located next to the **Number Format** drop down menu is the **Borders** button. Clicking this button will open a popup menu that allows you to put a border around one or more highlighted cells. Click a cell or highlight a group of cells, then Choose a border format or click advanced for more options.
Formulas		Clicking the Formulas button will open a popup menu so that you may choose from a variety of mathematical functions. The popup menu will provide a list of all the functions as well as a brief description of each and how to use them.
Auto Sum		Highlight a group of cells in a single column or row; then click the button. This automatically adds the values of all the highlighted cells and puts the result in the next available cell in that column or row.
Equals		This button allows you to edit formulas in the **Cell Text Field**.
Insert		This button lets you add individual cells and entire rows or columns to your current sheet.
Delete		This button lets you remove individual cells and entire rows or columns from you current sheet.
Merge		This button lets you combine multiple cells into a single cell. If you click a cell that has been merged then this button will change to an unmerge button. Clicking unmerge will return the previously merged cell into multiple smaller cells.
Cell Text Field		The white rectangle next to the equals sign is called the **Cell Text Field**. Here you can edit the text or formula that is in the cell you have selected.

Using Advanced Border Options:

1. Choose a color for your border from the color drop down menu.

2. Choose a line style for your border from one of the four style options located below

3. Select one or more lines that you want to add to your border with the color and style selections you have just made.

4. You can select different colors and styles for different lines to add or change current lines by repeating the previous steps.

5. A preview of your border is on the rightmost side of the popup window. If at any time you wish to start over you can click the **Clear** button located below the preview.

6. When you are done editing your border click **OK** to apply the border or **Cancel** to return to your spreadsheet without applying your border.

Quick Stats

At the bottom of the screen just above the slider are three *Quick Stats*: **Sum**, **Average**, and **Count**.

Sum

This number represents the total of the values of all highlighted cells. If a cell contains a non-numerical value, it will not be added to the sum.

Average

This number represents the average of all highlighted cells. If a cell contains a non-numerical value, it will not be included in the average. For example, if the cells highlighted contained: 7, 0, 11, a, and 2 then average would equal to $7 + 0 + 11 + 2 = 20 / 4 = 5$.

Count

This number counts how many cells are highlighted. If a cell is blank it will not be counted.

Sprint CapTel

Sprint® CapTel is a free, web-based service for individuals with hearing loss to read word-for-word captions of their phone calls on their computer. Users speak to the other person through any telephone, including cordless, landline or cell phones, AND read, on their computer, what the other person is saying. The best part is that there is NO special equipment required!

While the service is free, users must register to use the service. This is a simple process and will be explained below. You will need to have an email account to register for a Sprint CapTel account and use the Sprint CapTel application.

Overview

Sprint CapTel allows a person who has difficulty hearing over the phone to read word-for-word captions of their call. You can make or receive calls using your own cell phone, desk phone, cordless phone, or even an amplified phone. You can read captions of that call right here on the Sprint CapTel application on your computer. Specially trained Sprint agents use an enhanced voice recognition technology to caption your calls. All calls are kept secure and confidential. Captions are provided 24 hours a day, 7 days a week in English, and from 7am to 11pm Central Time, 7 days a week in Spanish.

How Does it Work?

The Sprint CapTel service provides a way for you to read what the other person on the phone is saying. The Sprint captioned telephone operator is on the phone with you and transcribes what the other person says for you to read.

1. You speak directly to the person you are conversing with

2. The other person speaks directly to you

3. The Sprint captioned telephone operator transcribes the other person's words into text that you can read using voice-recognition technology

4. You listen to the other person while reading the transcribed text of what they are saying on the screen

Register for a Sprint CapTel Account

Registering for a Sprint CapTel account requires having an email account. If you have an email account, you will be able to register by going to a website and completing a form. When the form is submitted, you will receive an email from Sprint CapTel to activate your account. If you do not have an email account, call our Support number for assistance.

To assist in registering for an account, you may want to print out this help page by clicking the print button at the top of this window. If you do not have a printer, you may want to write down the numbered instructions below for completing the registration form and the instructions for activating the account.

Complete the Registration Form:

1. Click *More*
2. Click *Sprint Cap Tel* - this takes you to a webpage
3. Click the "Register Now!" button on the webpage
4. Complete the form and write down the username and password you chose - you will need it each time you make or receive a call using the Sprint CapTel application.
5. When the form is completed, click the "Submit" button at the bottom of the form.
6. Click the *Close Popup* button at the bottom of the window to close it.

Once you complete and submit the registration form, you will need to activate your account.

Activate the Account

After you submit the registration form, you will receive an email from Sprint CapTel to activate your account. Check your email inbox for this email. When you receive it, click the link inside the email to activate your account.

Place a Call

Once you have activated your Sprint CapTel account, you may begin using the Sprint® CapTel application to place calls. Follow these instructions to place a call. You may want to print these instructions or write them down.

1. Click *More*
2. Click *Sprint CapTel*
3. Enter your username and password, in the fields provided and then click "Sign In".
4. Enter in your home phone number - or the number where you will be placing and receiving your calls - and then click the "Submit" button.
5. Type in the phone number of the person you are calling in the "Number to Dial" box.
6. Click "Place Call"
7. Sprint CapTel will dial your phone number first. Answer your phone when it rings.
8. Sprint CapTel will dial the number you are calling next.
9. The call center will caption what the other person says, and the text will appear on the computer screen for you to read.

Receive a Call

You can easily use the Sprint CapTel application on your computer to transcribe calls that you receive. Follow these instructions. You may want to print these instructions or write them down.

1. Click **More**
2. Click **Sprint CapTel**
3. Enter your username and password, in the fields provided and then click the "Sign In" button.
4. Enter in your home phone number - or the number where you will be placing and receiving your calls - and then click the "Submit" button.
5. You will be at the "Place Call" screen. On the right side, you will see "Waiting for calls at" and your phone number. You're ready to receive calls!
6. Tell your callers to dial 800-933-7219 first to connect to the call center, and then, when prompted, enter in your telephone number and press the pound sign: "#".
7. When your phone rings, answer it and begin speaking to your caller.
8. Captions of what your caller says will appear on the computer screen for you to read.

NOTE: If you log out you will not be able to receive incoming calls.

Getting Help

Frequently Asked Questions

Who do I contact for Sprint CapTel customer service?

Sprint CapTel customer service is currently available at:

- 1-888-269-7477 English
- 1-866-670-9134 Spanish
- E-mail: captel@captel.com

Customer service is 24 hours a day, closed on holidays. Calls or emails after hours will be responded to as soon as possible on the next business day.

I have not received my activation email yet

You can do a couple of things:

- Activation emails are normally sent fairly quickly after registration. However, in peak usage times, that email may become delayed. Please wait for up to one hour for that registration email to appear in your inbox.
- Check to be sure input the correct email address for your registration.
- Check your spam filters on your email address to ensure your email provider did not flag your registration email as spam.
- If all of the above fail to have the registration email appear, please contact CapTel customer service at 888-269-7477 or captel@captel.com. Live customer service will

be available 24/7 and closed holidays. Share with the representative what time, date, username and email address you used to register.

I forgot my username and/or password

If you have forgotten your username or password, follow these instructions:

1. Click **More**
2. Click **Sprint CapTel**
3. Click the "Forgot Password" link & enter the email address used to create your account.
4. Your username and password will be emailed to that email address.

Can I save my conversation?

Yes. To save a copy of your conversation, highlight the text of your conversation, copy the text to your computer's clipboard, and then paste into the **Write** application or into an email.

Is there a charge to use the service?

No. The service is free. You will not be charged to use the captioning service. The CapTel service is funded by the Interstate TRS Fund, overseen by the U.S. Federal Communications Commission (FCC).

Can I dial 911 with Sprint CapTel?

Yes. You can dial 911 Emergency Services using Sprint CapTel, however there are some things you need to know.

The fastest method of reaching help in an emergency is by dialing 911 directly from your phone. If you are able to communicate your location to the 911 operators, you will save valuable time by just dialing 911 directly on your telephone without the aid of captions. If you use Sprint CapTel to call 911, it is crucial that your correct address is listed in your Sprint CapTel user profile that you created when you registered for your Sprint CapTel account. If you cannot communicate your location, the 911 operator may use the address listed in your Sprint CapTel account to send help. If the address for your Sprint CapTel account is incorrect, 911 may not be able to send help. When you call 911 with Sprint CapTel, you must be able to tell the 911 operator your location. If you cannot communicate your location,

DO NOT USE Sprint CapTel FOR EMERGENCY CALLS. Instead, hang up and dial 911 directly from your telephone.

Can I call 411?

No. Sprint CapTel is designed to only accept 10 digit numbers at this time. Sprint is working on adding the feature of being able to call non-10 digit numbers.

Stopwatch

This is a stopwatch application used to record the duration of an event.

To use the Stopwatch:

- **Click the More button**
- **Click the Stopwatch icon**

Stopwatch Functions

Go

Click Go to start or resume the stopwatch. The button will change to read Pause.

Pause

Click Pause to stop a stopwatch.

Reset

Click Reset to set your stopwatch back to zero.

Using Multiple Stopwatches

Add Stopwatch

To create a new stopwatch, click Add Stopwatch. You can add up to four stopwatches at the same time.

Remove Stopwatch

Clicking Remove Stopwatch will remove the last stopwatch that you added.

Timer

This application contains a number of timers that you can use to set various alarms for.

The following instructions assume that you have:

- **Clicked on the More button**
- **Clicked on the Timer icon**

Using Timers

Set a Timer

You may create several timers. Follow these instructions to set a timer:

1. Use the arrow keys to set the amount of time you would like to count down from.
2. Enter a name for the timer using the Name field if you wish.

3. Click Go to start or resume the timer. The button will then change to a Pause button. Click Pause to stop the timer.

Reset a Timer

If a timer is paused or has run down to zero, then clicking Reset will set the timer to the previous set time. Clicking Reset before the timer is set will set the timer to the default time of **two minutes**.

Add a Timer

To create a new timer, click Add Timer

NOTE: You can set a maximum of 4 timers at once.

Remove a Timer

To remove the last timer added, click Remove Timer.

 # Write

This application allows you to create, edit, and view documents with a simple, easy-to-use word processor.

To use the Write application:

- **Click the More button**
- **Click the Write icon**

Write Functions

New	**Create a New File**	Click New to create a new, blank document. When you first open the Write application, a new, blank document is created for you.
Open	**Open Existing File**	Click Open to open an existing document. The File Browser window appears to help you find a document to open. If the document you want to open is in a folder, click the folder name to open the folder and list its contents. Once you find the document you want to open, click the name of the document, then click Open.
Save	**Save a Document**	Click **Save** to save the current document. The **File Browser** window appears the first time you save a document to help you find a place to store the new document. Click the white text field next to the

word **Name**, then type a name for your document. After you have chosen a name for your document, click the green *Save* button. It's a good idea to save your document periodically - even if you are not finished.

When saving documents, folders can be used to help organize your documents. The **New Folder** button in the file browser allows you to create a new folder. To create a new folder, click **New Folder**, type a name for your folder, click **Ok** and you'll see your new folder. To store a document in that folder, click the folder name, click **Open** to open the folder, then click **Save** to save the document in that folder.

 Save a Document under a new name

If you have already saved your document, you can also save it under a new name by pressing the *Save As* button, changing the file name, and pressing the *Save* button. Saving a document under a new name saves it as a new file and so leaves the original unchanged.

 **Close the Document**

Close the current document. You will be asked if you wish to save the document.

 Print a Document

Click to print the current document. You'll need to have a printer turned on and connected to your computer (see page 116). For more help with printers, click Settings, Printer Settings, then click Help.

Back **Go Back to More**

Click Back to close the Write application and go back to the More page of applications.

Deleting Documents

To Delete a document, open **File Manager**, see page 73, then using the left pane , locate the file you wish to delete, select the file, then click **Delete**.

Keyboard Controls

99

Functions like **Cut**, **Copy**, **Paste**, **Undo** and **Redo** can be utilized by using a combination of keystrokes from your keyboard. See pages 19 for the details.

NOTE: Keyboard Controls will only work a real keyboard; the on-screen keyboard will not work.

Toolbar Buttons

At the top of the Write application is a toolbar with buttons that provide helpful functions. Click the buttons in the toolbar to create different text effects or format your document. It's fun to experiment so be creative! Below is a list of toolbar buttons.

▼	**Font Type**	Drop down menu to display a list of font types. Select the font you like, and the text you type will be in that font.
14 ▼	**Font Size**	Drop down menu to display a list of font sizes. Select a size you like, and the text you type will be in that size.
A	**Font Color**	Click the **Font Color** button to display a list of font colors. Select a color you like, and the text you type will be in that color.
B	**Bold**	Creates **bold text**.
I	**Italic**	Creates *italic text*.
U	**Underline**	Creates <u>underlined text</u>.
≡	**Align Left**	Creates text aligned with the left margin of the cell.
≡	**Align Center**	Creates text that is centered between the side margins of the cell.
≡	**Align Right**	Creates text that is aligned with the right margin of the cell.
≡	**Justified**	Fills gaps between the words so that the text fits evenly between the margins. Similar to a newspaper column.
≔	**Ordered List**	Creates a numbered list of items.
≔	**Bulleted List**	Creates a bulleted list of items.
⇤≣	**Left Indent**	Decreases text indentation.
≣⇥	**Right Indent**	Increases text indentation.

Spell Check

When you are writing a document, you might notice that occasionally words are underlined with a jagged red line. This means that these words may be misspelled. You can right-click the underlined word to see possible corrections. Please be aware that the red line does not necessarily mean that a word IS misspelled but rather that it is not recognized by the computer. A common example of this is a person's last name.

Settings – Application Specific

Email Settings

The following instructions assume that you have:

- **Click the Email button**
- **Click the Settings button (located in the upper right corner of the screen)**

This page allows you to enter your email account credentials and settings in order to use the Email application. It is comprised of two sections, Account and Folders, which you can navigate between, using the buttons located on the right-hand side

Email Account Setup

Email Address/Password

An email account has an email address and password. An example of an email address is Cutie@GreenCity.com. Another example is WhiteKnight10@FireLight.net.

To configure your computer with your email account, enter your email address and the password into the provided fields and then click Save. The computer will attempt to connect to the email server. Once successful, you will see **Email Account Status: Connected**.

NOTE: In some cases (Yahoo and Gmail for example), you'll need to enable forwarding of POP or IMAP email by accessing your account's online (web) settings.

If you have any questions, call our support team and they will be happy to assist you.

Removing an Email Address

If you ever want to change or remove the email address that you have set up on your computer, click the Remove Account button. This will delete your email settings and all the email sent to this account. You may then enter a different email address if you wish.

Advanced Account Options

NOTE: Do not check the Show advanced options box unless you are familiar with advanced email protocol or unless instructed to do so by a trusted Tech Buddy or Customer Support. If you have changed settings unintentionally, click Reset to Defaults in order to reset your email settings to the default information.

The values for your email account settings are provided by your email host. If you are unsure of your email settings, you should contact your email host.

If you are having trouble setting up your email account and need further assistance, please call Customer Support.

Email Folder Settings

Existing Folders List

This page displays a list of all of your folders and allows you to manage your **Folder List**.

NOTE: Some folders are integral to your email and cannot be moved, renamed or deleted. You will receive a warning if you attempt to do so.

Add

This button lets you create new folders in which to store and organize your email. To create a new folder, follow these instructions:

1. Click Add.
2. A dialog box will appear asking you to enter a name for your new folder. Type a name in the text box, but be aware that it cannot be the same as an existing folder.
3. Click OK to create your new folder; however if you change your mind and no longer wish to create a folder, click Cancel.

Rename

This button lets you change the name of an existing folder. To rename an existing folder, follow these instructions:

1. Click the check box next to the folder you want to rename.
2. Click Rename.
3. A dialog box will appear asking you to enter a new name for your folder. Type a name in the text box, but be aware that it cannot be the same as an existing folder.
4. Click OK to rename your folder; however if you change your mind and no longer wish to rename this folder, click Cancel.

Remove

This button lets you delete a folder. To remove an existing folder, follow these instructions:

1. Click the check box next to the folder you want to remove
2. Click *Remove*
3. You will be asked to confirm your decision. Click *Yes* to delete the folder, or *Cancel* to cancel the operation

Move Up

This button lets you move the selected folder up in the folder list. To move a folder up, follow these instructions:

1. Click in the checkbox next to the folder you want to move up
2. Click Move Up

You will see the folder moved up one item in the list on the settings page. The changes will be reflected in the folder list. Tip: Put folders that you use most at the top.

Move Down

This button lets you move the selected folder down in the folder list. To move a folder down, follow these instructions:

1. Click in the checkbox next to the folder you want to move down
2. Click Move Down

You will see the folder moved down one item in the list on the settings page. The changes will be reflected in the Inbox folder list. Tip: Put folders that you use least at the bottom.

Email Options

Compose Options

This option allows you to show either the CC or BCC field while composing emails. These fields are used to organize your email recipients. CC stands for "Carbon Copy" and BCC stands for "Blind Carbon Copy". These terms originally applied to paper correspondence and now also apply to email.

Show CC

Selecting this option will show the CC field and hide the BCC field. CC refers to the practice of sending a message to multiple recipients where the recipients are organized into primary and secondary recipients. Primary recipients are entered into the To field and secondary recipients are entered into the CC field. Email recipients entered into the CC field will receive a copy of the email and their email addresses will be visible to all recipients of the email.

Show BCC

Selecting this option will hide the CC field and show the BCC field. BCC refers to the practice of sending a message to multiple recipients in a way that conceals some of the recipients. Email recipients entered in to the BCC field will receive a copy of the email; however, their email addresses will be concealed from all other recipients.

Web Browser Settings

Browser settings let you choose what kind of websites to allow or filter out. If you are the Primary user, you can regulate the web filter for guests and other users. Be aware that this will filter out most but not all websites in specific categories.

To view the Browser Settings:
- **Click the Web button**
- **Click the Settings button (located in the upper right corner of the screen)**

Settings

Default Zoom

This value is the default magnification setting for all your web pages. Try setting this value to 30%, then viewing your web pages to see if this is right for you. You may need to adjust this value to find a magnification that is right for you. The higher the value, the greater the magnification.

NOTE: If you are using magnification and are not seeing all content on a web page - or some items are hidden or not available - try setting your magnification to a lower setting. Some web pages do not work at higher magnifications. This is due to restrictions on the web page itself.

Home Page

This value defaults to Quick Links, the pre-defined page of shortcuts. To change your Web Browser's home page, enter the desired home page's address e.g. www.yahoo.comhere.

Enable Web Filter

This check box activates the web filter and lets you choose what to block. The options and descriptions are as follows:

- **Graphic Content** - This option blocks: adult content, art nudes, mixed adult, naturism/nudism, pornography, and sexuality.
- **Drugs and Alcohol** - This option blocks: beer & liquor information, beer & liquor sale, and drugs.
- **Online Shopping** - This option blocks: ecommerce, shopping, and online auctions.
- **Violence** - This option blocks: aggressive content, guns, violence, and weapons.
- **Gambling** - This option blocks: gambling.
- **Identity Protection** - This option blocks: sites that may attempt to gather your personal information or show unwanted pop-ups.

After choosing one or more of these options, you can click the Save button to save and activate the filter; however, if you change your mind and do not want to save the changes to the filter, simply click Cancel.

Primary User Options

If you are the **primary user**, you have extra options that allow you to set the filter for other users.

Select User

If there is more than one user on your device, this drop-down menu will appear. Using this drop-down menu, you can choose between users in order to set the filter for them. Additionally, you can use the Lock Settings: check box to prevent removing these settings.

Set as Default

Located to the left of the Save button is the Set As Default button. This button uses the currently selected filter options and activates them in **Guest Mode** & for newly created users.

Import Favorites (Bookmarks)

If you have favorites/bookmarks saved on your old PC or Mac computer, you can add them to your new computer by performing 3 general tasks:

    A. **Export** the favorites/bookmarks from the web browser on your old PC into a file.

    B. **Transfer** them to your new computer, either via email or a portable drive.

    C. Then use the ***Import Favorites*** button to add them to your new **Favorites**.

Instructions on how to export and transfer from your old computer are listed below. The following instructions are for the most recent version of the most popular web browsers: Internet Explorer & Mozilla Firefox. If you are not using these browsers or have any questions about this procedure, please don't hesitate to call support.

    A. Exporting favorites into a file

Listed below are the instructions for exporting Favorites/Bookmarks for Internet Explorer or Firefox. When you have finished exporting your Favorites, go to the section labeled

Transferring for PC.

      Exporting from Internet Explorer

1. Open ***Internet Explorer*** on your old PC
2. Click the **Favorites (Star)** button on the upper right.
3. Click the down arrow to the right of the **Add to Favorite** button.
4. Click on **Import and export...**
5. Click **Export to a file**, then Click **Next.**
6. Click the check box for **Favorites**, and then click **Next.**

7. Select the Favorites folder that you want to export. If you want to export all Favorites, select the top level Favorites folder. Otherwise, select the individual folder that you want to export.
8. Click **Next.**
9. By default, Internet Explorer will save the file as **bookmark.htm** in your Documents folder. If you want to use a name other than bookmark.htm, or if you want to store the exported Favorites in a folder other than the Documents folder, go to step 10. If not, skip to step 12.
10. Click **Browse**. Then choose a new file name and/or storage location.
11. When you have chosen a new file name and/or storage location, click **Save**.
12. Click **Export**.
13. Click **Finish**.

Exporting from Mozilla Firefox
1. Open *Mozilla Firefox* on your old PC.
2. Click the **Bookmarks** menu option on the left side of the navigation toolbar.
3. Click the **Show All Bookmarks** option.
4. When the popup loads, click the **Import and Backup** menu option.
5. From the drop-down menu, click **Export Bookmarks to HTML...**.
6. By default, Mozilla Firefox will save the file as **bookmarks.html** in your Downloads folder. If you want to use a name other than bookmarks.html, or if you want to store the exported Favorites in a folder other than the Downloads folder, type a different name and/or change the storage location. If not, skip this step.
7. Click **Save**.

Saving Favorites in a Mac
The **Firefox** instructions are the same as the PC, for **Safari** browsers:
1. Open *Safari* on your Mac and click the **File** menu option.
2. Click the **Export Bookmarks...** menu option.
3. By default, Safari will save the file as **bookmarks.html** in your Documents folder. If you want to use a name other than bookmarks.html, or if you want to store the exported Favorites in a folder other than the Documents folder, type a different name and/or change the storage location. If not, skip this step.
4. Click **Save**.

B. Transferring the file to your new computer

Now that you have your Favorites saved as a file, you can transfer them to your new computer by **Email** or using a **USB compatible portable drive**. The instructions for each method are listed below. When you have finished transferring your Favorites file, go to the section labeled **Import Favorites using the Import Favorites Button**.

Transferring via Email (PC & Mac)

1. On your PC/Mac, open your web browser.
2. Go to the website of your email provider. For example, if you have your email address were xxxxxxxx@gmail.com, you would go to www.gmail.com.
3. Open a new email, and put your email address in the **To:** field.
4. Attach your Favorites file to the email and send it.
5. On your new computer, go to the *Email* application.
6. Open the email you just sent to yourself. If the email is not present in your Inbox, click the **Refresh Mail** button.
7. Once you have opened the email, click the **View Attachments** button.
8. When the attachment viewer loads, click the **Save** button.
9. When the Save File popup loads, click the **Save** button.

Transferring via USB

1. Move the file from your old computer to your USB device. If you do not know how to do this, it is recommended that you either search Google for instructions or ask for assistance from a friend or relative.
2. Once the file is on the USB device, safely remove it from your old computer and insert it into a USB port on your new computer.
3. Click **More**.
4. Click **File Manager**.
5. Click on the **USB** folder in the **From** panel.
6. Find file you just moved onto the USB device and click on it.
7. In the **To** panel, click on the **Documents** folder.
8. Click **Move**.

C. Import Favorites using the Import Favorites Button

Now that you have your Favorites file saved on your computer, follow these instructions to import them to the Web application's Favorites page:

1. Click the **Web** button on the left side of the screen.
2. Click the **Settings** button, located in the upper righthand corner of the screen.
3. Click the **Import Favorites** button, in the upper righthand corner of the page.
4. A dialog box will appear on the screen telling you that you must have the bookmarks file saved on your computer and asking you if you wish to proceed. Click **Yes**.
5. Click the **Documents** folder.
6. Find the Favorites file and click on it.
7. After selecting the favorites file, click the **Open** button.
8. A dialog box shows that your favorites have been successfully imported.

After you Favorites have been successfully imported, you can access them via the Favorites button in the Web application.

Wiping the Browser Cache and Cookies

As you navigate to different websites, these websites may store pieces of information on your computer, called cookies, so that they can do things like load faster or remember that you were logged in.

Wipe Cache

Sometimes if you have problems with a website, it may ask you to clear the cache or cookies. To do this, simply press the **Wipe Cache** button. This will delete all cached information and "cookies" from your web browser. Any websites that you were logged into will now "forget" that you were logged in and you will have to login again the next time you visit the website.

Settings – General

To view General Settings…

- **Click on the Home button**
- **Click on the Settings button (located in the upper right corner of the screen)**

My Profile Settings

To view your Profile…

- **Click on the Home button**
- **Click on the Settings button (located in the upper right corner of the screen)**
- **Click on My Profile**

Enter Profile Information

Click in the space next to any of the following fields to enter or update your profile information. When you are finished, click Save Changes. If you do not want to keep the change(s), click Cancel Changes.

First Name - Enter your first name in this field.

Last Name - Enter your last name in this field.

Phone Number - Enter your phone number in this field.

Address 1, 2, and 3 - Enter your street address in these fields.

City - Enter the name of your city in this field.

State/Province - Enter the name of your state or province in this field.

Zip Code - Enter your zip code in this field. This updates the Weather location.

Birthday - Click each of the droplists to select the day, month, and year.

Anniversary - Click the droplists to select the day, month, and year of your anniversary.

Profile Picture - Click Change Picture to change your default profile picture. A popup window will open to allow you to choose a photo from one of your albums. Click the album containing the photo you want for your profile, click the photo, and then click OK. You can also take a picture using the built-in camera by following these instructions:

1. Click the **Use Camera** button.

2. A small preview window will appear. Use this window to decide how you want to appear in your photo.
3. When you are ready to take the picture, click the green **Take Picture** button, located above the preview window.
4. Upon clicking the **Take picture** button, a count down from 3 will begin and then your picture will be taken.
5. If you are satisfied with the photo, click **Done**. If not, simply reposition yourself and start over from step 3.
6. After clicking **Done**, your photo will be available in the **Profile** photo album (to view it in the Photos application click **Photos**, then click **My Albums**), look for the album labeled **Profile**.

System Info

This page lets you view status information about your computer.

To view your System Information:

- **Click the Home button**
- **Click the Settings button (located in the upper right corner of the screen)**
- **Click the System Info button**

Status information

This section displays basic information about the services to which your computer connects, including information such as the network connection status and status of any accounts you have configured.

A connected icon: ⊘ indicates an account is logged in - or a good connection.

A disconnected icon: ⊗ indicates that an account may not be configured - or that there may be a problem with this setting.

Get VIP Backup and Support

If you are not subscribed to VIP Backup and Support then the **Get VIP Backup and Support** button will appear. Clicking this button will cause a popup to appear where you can subscribe to this fee-based, monthly service. The benefits of VIP Backup and Support are:

1. Priority Calling: When you call our customer support line, your calls will be answered more quickly and with higher priority.
2. Network Backup: Your data is backed up to our servers safely and securely.

3. Remote Access Support: We can connect to your computer and see what you see in order to provide support and tutorials.

Update

The Update button is used to initiate a manual software update. You may be asked by Customer Service to click this button. Your computer will automatically check for updated software, so you will normally not need to click this button. Remember, all software updates are free!

Restart

The Restart button is used to restart your computer. Clicking Restart will reboot your computer and use any new software that was downloaded to your computer during your last session.

Start Logging

Press this button if directed by one of our support technicians, this directs your computer to temporarily record more detailed error messages, helping them to investigate certain issues.

System Information

Below the status information, you will see information about your computer. This section is mostly useful to Customer Support, specifically, the Device ID and User ID.

System Messages

At the bottom of the page, is a blank area that is used to display system messages from your computer. If you initiate a software update by clicking the Update button, you will see the system message, "Manual Software Update Started" and the date and time. Similarly, when a software update has been installed, this message will be displayed: "New software has been installed". This section will usually remain empty. If you receive a system message, a notice will appear in the Notices section of the Home screen. Clicking the notice will take you to this page to view the system message.

System Settings

This page lets you adjust personalized settings for your computer.

The following instructions assume that you have:
- **Click the Home button**
- **Click the Settings button (located in the upper right corner of the screen)**
- **Click the System Settings button**

Time Zone ▽

Click the droplist to select your local time zone.

Set Time

The time on your computer will be automatically set whenever you are connected to the internet; however if you are not connected to the internet, a Set Time button will appear and allow you to set the time manually.

Use Built-in Speakers ✓

Check this box to enable the built-in speakers.

Uncheck this check box to deactivate the built-in speakers so that you can plug in external speakers or headphones.

Use External Microphone ✓

Check this box: to enable or uncheck to disable the use of an external microphone.

Screen Saver ▽

Use the droplist button to choose a screen saver. You can choose from a slideshow of your favorite photos or a blank screen that will read "Touch Here!". If you do not want a screen saver, select None.

NOTE: The touchscreen on this computer does not experience "burn-in" and a screen saver is not required.

Idle Time ▽

This is the period of inactivity that occurs before the screen saver you have selected will begin. Use the droplist to select an idle time from 2 minutes up to 2 hours.

Enable Screen Lock

Checking this box will require you to enter your password before you can use your computer after a screen saver has started. This setting will be disabled if you have not set a password on your account.

Automatic Logout

Checking this box will cause your computer to automatically log you out if your computer is idle for the amount of time that you select from the droplist. ▽

Mouse Settings

This page lets you personalize your mouse. You can:

- Switch from a right-handed mouse to a left-handed mouse or back, see **Buttons**
- Select how fast the pointer follows as you move the mouse, see **Acceleration**
- Select the Color and Size of the mouse pointer, see **Cursor**

Print Settings

This page allows you to view and configure printers and print requests.

To view the Printer Settings

- **Click the Home button**
- **Click the Settings button (located in the upper right corner of the screen)**
- **Click the Print Settings Button**

Printers

Currently, the computer supports many **inkjet** printers from Hewlett Packard (HP). The printer must be connected directly to the computer with a USB printer cable. If the printer has memory card slots, you will be able to view and download photos just like you can with cards connected directly to the computer. If the printer has a scanning feature, you will be able to scan pictures into the computer. The *Scanner* application is available in the *More* section. At this time, faxing is not supported through the computer. You may fax directly from the printer.

Note: At this time the faxing feature of all-in-one printers is not supported. Faxing may be done directly through the printer.

USB Connections

The printer must be connected directly to the computer with a USB printer (A/B) cable. The rectangular end of the cable, which looks like those on the keyboard and mouse, should be plugged into any USB connector on the left side of the computer. The square end of the cable plugs into the printer, usually in the back.

Recommended Models

We sell the following printers; however, your computer supports a wide variety of HP printers. Please call us if you would like us to check a specific printer model for you.

- HP Deskjet 1112 – simple color printer
- HP Officejet 3830 – all-in-one color printer, copier and scanner

Supported Printers

If you would like to see if your printer is compatible with your computer, enter this URL into your browser address bar and click GO: https://developers.hp.com/hp-linux-imaging-and-printing/supported_devices/index Then follow these instructions:

1. While holding the Ctrl key down, tap the F key, this brings up the Search window
2. Type into that window your printer's type and model number, e.g. Officejet 3830.
3. You will then see the first instance of the lines matching that entry.

HP DeskJet Ink Advantage 3836 All-in-one Printer	3.15.7	No	Full
HP OfficeJet 3834 All-in-one Printer	3.15.7	No	Full
HP OfficeJet 3830 All-in-one Printer	3.15.7	No	Full
HP DeskJet Ink Advantage 1110 Printer Compatibility	3.15.7	No	Full
HP DeskJet 1111 Printer	3.15.7	No	Full

4. On that line, after the Name of the printer is an entry for the **Minimum HPLIP version**. Make note of that number. Then on your computer, Click Settings/Print Settings, you will see **Currently your computer only supports HP Printer (3.XX.YY)** where XX and YY represent the Year and Month of the release. e.g. 3.17.10 indicates your computer will support any HP printer with drivers released in Oct, 2017 or earlier. If the computer indicates higher number (a later date) then what is in the table, then the drivers are compatible so continue to step 5.
5. Check the next entry in the table, this is the **Driver plug-in**. If you see the word **No** then continue to step 6; otherwise your printer is not compatible with your computer.
6. Check the next entry in the table, this is the **Support level**. If you see the word **Full** then it is Fully compatible. Otherwise your printer is not fully compatible with your computer. Call our Technical support team at 800-730-6893 for help.

Printer Information
Printer Name
On the left side of the screen, you will see the name of any printer that was connected to the computer's USB port and powered on. If you just connected a printer, it could take a minute before the printer appears.

Print Test Page
This button will appear whenever your printer is ready to print. Clicking this button will print out a letter sized page after a short delay. Use this to verify your computer is talking to the printer and your printer is functioning normally.

Printer Status

On the right side of the screen, you will see the printer's current status. A change in the status may not appear immediately.

Printer is Ready

This indicates the printer is ready for printing and not currently printing anything.

Printer Not Ready

This indicates the printer is not ready for printing. There are several things you can check to fix this problem:

- The printer is turned on.
- The USB printer cable is plugged in to both the printer and computer.
- The paper is loaded into the printer.
- There are no errors on the printer. Errors may be shown on its display or indicated by a red or flashing light. Please follow the instructions on the display or consult the printer's User Manual to clear any error conditions.

Working on 1 Print Request

This will appear if you had recently tried printing something and it has not finished printing yet. It may also appear if you had been printing something and the printer was turned off or disconnected from the computer before printing was complete. A number greater than one (1) indicates you started to print a second item before the first item completed printing. It is ok to continue to use the computer while your items are being printed.

Cancel Print Request

This button will appear if you have one or more print requests being worked on. Clicking the button will cancel the oldest print request being worked on.

You may want to cancel a print request if it does not look the way you expected. You may also want to cancel a print request if it had been canceled at the printer first, or the printer was disconnected or turned off during printing.

If the printer was disconnected or turned off, cancel before re-connecting or turning on the printer. Otherwise, the printer may start printing immediately or print incorrectly.

NOTE: Any information that has already been sent to the printer will continue to print. Please use the printer's cancel button to cancel printing anything that had already been sent to the printer. If there were any problems performing the cancel, the next item may not print correctly.

Print Request Settings

This is the popup that appears when you want to print. This allows you to choose a few printing options.

Page Orientation

On the left-hand side of this popup are the Page Orientation checkboxes. These checkboxes are **Portrait**, which means that the vertical edge is longer than the horizontal edge, and **Landscape**, which means that the horizontal edge is longer than the vertical edge.

Copies:

This field lets you choose how many times the selection will be printed.

Print Page(s):

This field lets you select which pages you want to be printed.

Print Selection Only?

Click this checkbox if you want only the portion you've selected/highlighted to be printed.

Network Settings

This page allows you to connect to the Internet and view some of your network settings.

To view the Network Settings:

- **Click the Home button**
- **Click the Settings button (located in the upper right corner of the screen)**
- **Click the Network Settings button**

Network Interface Diagram

The diagram at the top of the screen shows how your computer is currently connected to the Internet. From left to right, it illustrates the connection from your computer to your modem or router, and then from your modem/router to the Internet. A successful connection from your computer to the Internet will display two green connected icons: ⊘. If at either point you see a red disconnected: ⊗, then you are having a problem connecting to your network.

The Test Network button will display the speeds at which information is being sent back and forth between your computer and the Internet, and also the strength of your wireless network if you are connected to a wireless network (WiFi).

IP address

You will also notice a string of numbers (ex. 192.168.1.1) below the picture of the computer. This is known as an **IP address**. It will only display when your computer is successfully connected to a network. Lack of an IP address can be an indicator of a possible problem connecting to the Internet. This number can change over time.

Network Interfaces

Below the network interface diagram, you will see two tables that represent the two interfaces that can be used to connect to the Internet, Wired Network and Wireless Network(s).

Wired Network

To connect to a wired network, you will need an Ethernet cable. You should have received one with your computer. This cable is similar to a phone cable, but the connector is wider. Like a phone cable, there is a little plastic tab that should click when plugged in. The plastic tab also needs to be pressed to remove the cable. If the tab is broken or missing, the cable will not stay in reliably.

Connecting this cable is simple. One end of the cable plugs in to the network port at the back of your computer. To locate the network port, refer to the **Quick Start Guide**, page 6 of this document. The other end of the cable plugs into the modem provided by your Internet provider, or, if you are using one, a router. The modem/router may have multiple ports. Any of the empty ports marked as wired, Ethernet, local, or LAN (Local Area Network) can be used. **DO NOT** use the single port marked Internet or modem. This single port is for use by your Internet provider. If you received two boxes from your Internet provider, use the box that is not connected directly to the wall.

Wireless Network(s)

Your computer is enabled to use a wireless (WiFi) network. If you would like to use WiFi, you will need to either have or purchase a wireless router at your local electronics store. Alternately, the modem provided by your Internet Provider may be configured to be a wireless network. In the Wireless Network(s) table, you will see all of the wireless networks that are available to your computer.

Understanding the Network Interface Tables

Both the Wired Network and Wireless Network(s) tables contain multiple columns of information to help you easily see information about that network.

Network name

The first column in each table displays the Name of the network. Only those with the strongest signals are shown. This information updates periodically.

MAC Address

This address uniquely identifies the box given to you by your Internet Provider. If multiple networks have the same name, this address can be used to determine which is yours. The address may appear on the side or bottom of the box.

Security Type (wireless only)

Your computer supports the following security types in order from strongest to weakest: WPA2/AES, WPA/TKIP, WEP, and None. Variations of these types, such as WEP64, are also supported. The security should have been set by your Internet provider and may be indicated on the side or bottom of the box.

Signal Strength (wireless only)

Many things affect the signal strength of a wireless network and the strength will fluctuate. Your neighbor's network could actually appear stronger. If you try changing anything to improve the signal strength, you must keep it that way for a minute to see whether it made things better or worse.

- Walls and furniture between the computer and the box given to you from your Internet provider can reduce the signal strength. Try to have a clear line of sight between them.

- The box given to you by your Internet provider has an internal or external antenna. Try pointing the antenna in different directions, rotating the box, or laying the box on its side.
- Cordless phones can have an adverse effect on your signal. Don't have a cordless phone right next to your Internet provider's box or the computer.

Status

The last column in each table displays the connection status for that network interface. You can have both types of interfaces connected at the same time, but the wired connection is generally faster and will be chosen automatically if both types are available.

The currently connected networks in either table will display a green connected icon:

.

Connecting Wirelessly

In the Status column of the Wireless Network(s) table, you will notice Connect buttons that allow you to connect to any of the wireless networks available to your computer. You can only be connected to one wireless network at a time.

Connect to your Wireless Network

1. Determine which of the networks shown is your network. Your wireless network name should have been given to you by your Internet Provider. It may also be written on the side or bottom of the box given to you by your Internet provider. In most cases, your home network should appear at the top of the list since it will most likely have the strongest signal.

2. Click the Connect button next to your network.

3. A pop-up window will appear showing you the network's information. You will be asked for any additional information if it is needed.

4. Click Ok.

NOTE: It could take several minutes to connect to a wireless network.

Passwords

A password may also be called passphrase or key. Sometimes, the name of a hidden network is also referred to as a password. If a password is needed, it should have been given to you by your Internet Provider. The password may also be written on the side or bottom of the box given to you by your Internet Provider. For the "WEP security type", it may be indicated as "WEP KEY" on the box.

Tech Buddy Settings

This page lets you create and manage a Tech Buddy.

To get to the Tech Buddy account page:

- **Click the Home button**
- **Click the Settings button**
- **Click the Tech Buddy button**

Tech Buddy is a great feature that allows a family member or trusted friend to provide you with remote assistance - from anywhere! When your Tech Buddy connects to your computer remotely, they'll be able to see your computer screen and control the mouse and keyboard. This can be very useful if you need a little extra guidance and/or are having difficulty describing what you're seeing on your computer.

To use the Tech Buddy feature, there are three basic steps:

1. Create a Tech Buddy Account - you will do this on your computer.
2. Install the Remote Access Software - your Tech Buddy will do this on their computer.
3. Run a Remote Session - your Tech Buddy will do this on their computer.

Since some of these steps must be performed by your Tech Buddy, it is advisable to print out this page and give it to them.

To print this page, click the Print button: .

Create a Tech Buddy Account

The Tech Buddy account will be used by your Tech Buddy. The account consists of a username, a password and an email address. You will create the account, and then give the information to your Tech Buddy.

To create a Tech Buddy account, follow these instructions:

1. Click Settings
2. Click Tech Buddy
3. Enter a username and a password
   Username Rules

   - o Must not have any spaces
   - o Must be between 8-16 characters

   Password Rules

   - o Must not have any spaces
   - o Must be between 8-16 characters
   - o Must have at least one number
   - o Must have at least one uppercase letter
   - o Must be different than the username.

4. Enter your Tech Buddy's email address - this is NOT your email address

5. Click Save.

You will need to give your Tech Buddy the username and password that you just created.

Install the Remote Access Software

Your Tech Buddy will need the username and password in order to complete this step. Have your Tech Buddy follow these instructions to install the software:

1. Go to www.telikin.com.

2. Click the "Tech Buddy" link in the top right corner of the screen.

3. Enter the Tech Buddy username and password and click "Log In".

4. **Windows:** click "Download Windows Tech Buddy", and follow the installation instructions.

5. **MAC:** select "Download MAC VNC Viewer", and follow the installation instructions.

Run a Remote Session

Once your Tech Buddy has installed the remote access software, have them follow these instructions to establish a remote connection to your computer:

Windows

1. Start the Tech Buddy Helper application.

2. Click Connect

3. Enter your Tech Buddy username and password.

4. Click Ok

The remote session will start and a window will open. The window will show you the machine you are connecting to and you can then use your mouse and keyboard to control it. To close the remote session, click the X in the top right corner of the window.

MAC

1. Start the Chicken of the VNC application.

2. Go to www.telikin.com; click the "Tech Buddy" link in the top right corner of the screen.

3. Enter your Tech Buddy username and password and click "Log In".

4. Follow the instructions to get the **IP Address**, **Port Number** and **Session Password**...

5. Enter that information into Chicken of the VNC and connect.

The remote session will start and a window will open. The window will show you the machine you are connecting to and you can then use your mouse and keyboard to control it. To close the remote session, click the X in the top right corner of the window.

Allow Unacknowledged Support

By checking this box, your Tech Buddy will be able to remotely access your computer without your permission.

NOTE: Do not check this box unless your Tech Buddy is a trusted friend or family member.

User Accounts Settings

This page lets you configure and manage the user accounts for your computer.

The following instructions assume that you have:

- **Clicked on the Home button**
- **Clicked on the Settings button (located in the upper right corner of the screen)**
- **Clicked on Users**

A user account is a way to control access to your computer. If you create a user account, you can lock your computer by logging out. You will also be asked to login to your computer each time you turn it on. To get more help on how to login/logout, click the Home button, and then click **Help**.

Here are some examples of scenarios where user accounts are useful:

- Two members of the household each have their own email account and want to use the same computer, but access their email accounts separately. Two user accounts would be created; one for each person.

- Guests are coming over and you want them to be able to use the internet on your computer, but don't want them to see your email - or other important data on your computer. One user account would be created, and you would log out of your account when you have visitors, putting the computer into Guest Mode.

If you are the only person using your computer and/or do not need to protect your data, then you most likely do not need to create a user account.

Types of Accounts

You can create up to three user accounts on your computer. There are two different kinds of user accounts that can be created:

- Primary Account - your computer can only have one primary user account. The person logged into the primary user account can create and manage secondary accounts. A primary user account must be created before secondary user accounts can be created.

- Secondary Account - your computer can have up to two secondary accounts. The person logged into a secondary user account can only manage their own account.

Guest Mode

Once you create a user account, you can easily put your computer into Guest Mode by logging out of your account. Guest mode will disable certain features of your computer, while allowing access to the internet via the Web button. The following features will be disabled while in Guest Mode:

- Video Chat
- Email
- Photos
- Calendar
- Contacts

Managing Accounts

Create a Primary User Account

The first user account you create is the called the primary user account. All other accounts created are called secondary accounts. A primary user account must be created before any secondary user accounts can be created.

As the primary user, you will be able to create and manage secondary (other) user accounts. Secondary users can only manage their own accounts.

To create the primary account, please do the following:

1. Click Settings. If you were on the **Home** page, skip to step 3.
2. Click General Settings.
3. Click Users
4. Enter the desired username in the Current User: field. Here are the rules for creating a username:

   - must be 8-45 characters long
   - must start with a letter
   - must be only letters and numbers
   - must not contain spaces

1. Optional: A password is not required. If you want to create a password for your account, then enter your desired password in the Password: and Verify Password fields. Here are the rules for creating a password.

   - is case sensitive (capital letters and small letters matter)
   - must be 8-16 characters
   - must not contain spaces
   - must contain at least one UPPER CASE letter
   - must contain at least one number

2. Optional: Choose one or two security questions and enter the answers. You will be asked the security questions if you forget your password.

3. Click Save
4. Write down the username and password (if you have created one) for the primary account

If you have a password set up for your account and have the screen lock enabled, it is recommended that you set up two security questions that you can answer, so you can login if you forget your password.

Create a Secondary User Account

Only the primary user may create secondary accounts. To create a secondary account, you must be logged into the primary user account. Once logged in, please do the following:

1. Click Settings. If you were on the Home page, skip to step 3.
2. Click General Settings
3. Click Users
4. Click Add User
5. Enter the desired username in the Username: field. Here are the rules for creating a username:
   - must be 8-45 characters long
   - must start with a letter
   - must be only letters and numbers
   - must not contain spaces
6. Optional: A password is not required. If you want to create a password for your account, then enter your desired password in the Password: and Verify Password fields. Here are the rules for creating a password.
   - is case sensitive (capital letters and small letters matter)
   - must be 8-16 characters
   - must not contain spaces
   - must contain at least one UPPER CASE letter
   - must contain at least one number
7. Click Save
8. Write down the username and password (if you have created one) for the secondary account

Once the secondary user account is created, the person can log into their account and enter their security questions; however it is completely optional.

Delete a Secondary User Account

You must be logged in to the primary user account to delete secondary user accounts. To delete a secondary user account, please do the following:

1. Click Settings. If you were on the Home page, skip to step 3
2. Click General Settings
3. Click Users
4. From the Manage User droplist, select the user you want to delete
5. Click Remove User.
6. When the dialog box will appear saying, "Are you sure you wish to remove this user", click Yes.

Change Account Username/Password/Questions

When you are logged in, you can change your username, password and/or security questions at any time.

If you have a password set up for your account and have the screen lock enabled, it is recommended that you set up two security questions that you can answer, so you can login if you forget your password.

To make changes to your user account, please do the following:

1. Click Settings. If you were on the Home page, skip to step 3.
2. Click General Settings
3. Click Users - your account information will appear at the top of the screen
4. You may change your username, password and/or security questions, and then click Save to save your changes

If you are logged into the primary user account, you can only change the username and/or password for secondary accounts. The secondary user can create/change their security questions by logging into their user account, then following the instructions to Change Account Username/Password/Questions. To change the username/password for a secondary account, please do the following:

1. Click Settings. If you were on the Home page, skip to step 3.
2. Click General Settings
3. Click Users
4. From the Manage User droplist, select the user you want to edit
5. You may change the username/password, and then click Save to save your change

Warranty & End User License Agreement (EULA)

Telikin Standard Product Warranty

General Terms and Conditions -Venture 3 Systems LLC., hereunder "V3", offers a Twelve (12) months limited warranty on Telikin computers, All-in-one PCs, hereunder "Product" from the original date of purchase. The limited warranty is under no circumstances transferable to any other party that is not the original buyer of the Product. This limited warranty only covers the Product that is purchased in the United States and Canada.

Venture 3 Systems LLC (V3) will repair or by any other efforts restore the defective Product to its working condition as originally configured by V3. V3 is not responsible for any subsequent installation by any third party or by the owner. V3 may provide refurbished equipment to restore product to original working condition.

Limited Warranty - Within the valid limited warranty period applied to the Product, Customer may contact V3 for warranty service only when the Product purchased becomes defective under proper usage, the limited warranty is under no circumstances transferable to any other party that is not the original buyer of the Product. The limited warranty DOES NOT cover Cosmetic damages, damage or loss to, data, or removable storage media, or damage due to the following;

1.   Acts of God, accident, misuse, abuse, negligence, commercial use or modifications of the Product;
2.   Improper operation or maintenance of the Product;
3.   Connection to improper voltage supply;
4.   Attempted or unauthorized repair by any party other than V3.
5.   The warranty seals have been broken or altered.

The limited warranty DOES NOT apply when the malfunction results from the use of the Product in conjunction with accessories, products or ancillary or peripheral equipment, or where it is determined by V3 that there is no fault with the Product itself.

V3 is ONLY responsible for the Telikin branded product purchased in the United States and Canada. The limited warranty service is not, in any way, applicable for any OS or software configured in the Product. Customer's dated sales receipt, showing the original date of purchase of the product is customer's proof of purchase. Customer may be requested by V3 to provide the proof of purchase of the Product when attempting to make use of the limited warranty service.

The following items (inclusive but not limited to) are covered under this warranty.

CPU, HDD, MEMORY, MOTHERBOARD, TOUCH SCREEN, SPEAKERS, DVD/CD, LCD PANEL, WIRELESS MODULE, MICROPHONE, WEBCAM, POWER ADAPTER, KEYBOARD, MOUSE.

Accessories (inclusive but not limited to), such as keyboard and mouse, are not covered by warranty, except DOA (Dead on arrival). Claims for DOA keyboards, or mice must be submitted within 1 month of purchase date.

Labor - Within the limited warranty period applied to the Product, V3 will repair defects in the Product at no charge. After the limited warranty period applied to the Product, Customer can choose to have the Product repaired on a fee basis. The Customer may also choose to purchase an extended warranty. See Extended warranty terms.

Parts - Within the limited warranty period applied to the Product, V3 will repair or replace the defective parts of the Product. After the limited warranty period applied to the Product, Customer can choose to have the parts of the Product to be repaired or replaced on a fee basis. The Customer may also choose to purchase an extended warranty. See Extended warranty terms.

Protection / Back-Up of Stored Data - Unless the Customer has purchased the VIP Support program, which includes automatic network backup, it is Customer's responsibility to back up the contents of your hard drive, including any data you have stored on the hard drive. The VIP Support program can be purchased directly from your Telikin computer by going to "MORE", "BACKUP/RESTORE", and pressing the "Sign Up Now" button, or by calling 1-800-730-6893.

IF DURING THE REPAIR OF THE PRODUCT THE CONTENTS OF THE HARD DRIVE ARE ALTERED, DELETED, OR IN ANYWAY MODIFIED, V3 IS NOT RESPONSIBLE WHATSOEVER. CUSTOMER'S PRODUCT WILL BE RETURNED AS ORIGINALLY CONFIGURED WHEN MANUFACTURED/PURCHASED.

Optional Extended Warranty –The 2 Year Extended Warranty covers the Telikin for 2 years from the date of purchase.

How to Purchase an Extended Warranty - All end users who purchase Telikin computers must register products prior to purchasing the extended warranty. You can register your product from the "Please register your Product" notice in the 'Notices' panel on the "HOME" page. Once valid serial numbers are entered during product registration, end users will be eligible to purchase the extended warranty. This warranty policy DOES NOT apply to accessories such as Keyboard, mice, external speakers, headphones, and printers.

The Following items (inclusive but not limited to) are covered under this warranty.

CPU, HDD, MEMORY, MOTHERBOARD, TOUCH SCREEN, SPEAKERS, DVD/CD, LCD PANEL, WIRELESS MODULE, MICROPHONE, WEBCAM and POWER ADAPTER, KEYBOARD, MOUSE.

Terms and Conditions:

The Warranty Extension Service must be purchased within the 90 days of the original purchase date. (The purchase invoice or other proof of purchase is required.) The Warranty Extension Service DOES NOT cover Cosmetic damages (scratches, dents…etc.), lost, stolen, incorrect or inadequate custom installation, intentional damage, recovery or transfer data, act of God or nature.

The Warranty Extension Service only covers failures or malfunctions that occur during the warranty period and under normal use conditions, as well as any material or workmanship defects. The warranty will not apply if:

The user is unable to provide proof of warranty and/or proof of purchase

The warranty seals have been broken or altered

The product has been tampered, repaired and/or modified by non-Venture 3 Systems (V3) Service Technician.

Damages due to use outside of the operation or storage parameters or environment detailed in the Quick Start Guide, or built-in HELP files or Videos.

The serial number on the Telikin has been altered, cancelled or removed

Damage caused by improper installation or improper connection to a peripheral device

Damage caused by accident, natural disaster, intentional or accidental misuse, abuse, neglect or improper maintenance, or use under abnormal conditions

Damages resulting from a malicious network attack or Virus.

The Warranty Extension Service can only be purchased and applies to products purchased in the United States and Canada.

V3 will only cover the one-way ground shipping from the point of service back to the user's location.

Extended Warranty is non-transferable to any other party that is not the original buyer of the Product.

Extended Warranty purchase is NOT refundable.

Customer must contact V3 technical support and obtain a RA number from V3 prior to returning the defective Product. Customer needs to return the defect Product to V3 within 15 days from the RA issuance date. Failing to do so may prevent customer from being eligible for the issued RA number and thus Customer may need to request another RA number.

In the case of specific part which is no longer manufactured, the then current closest functionally equivalent Replacement Equipment will be used as determined by the V3 technician.

End User License Agreement (EULA)

IMPORTANT: PLEASE READ THE TERMS AND CONDITIONS OF THIS LICENSE AGREEMENT CAREFULLY BEFORE USING THIS PRODUCT. Venture 3 Systems LLC ("Company") End-User License Agreement ("EULA") is a legal agreement between you (either an individual or a single entity) and Company for SOFTWARE identified above which may include associated software components, media, videos, printed materials, and "online" or electronic documentation ("SOFTWARE"). By installing, copying, or otherwise using the SOFTWARE, you agree to be bound by the terms of this EULA. This license agreement represents the entire agreement concerning the program between you and Company, (referred to as "licenser"), and it supersedes any prior proposal, representation, or understanding between the parties. If you do not agree to the terms of this EULA, do not install or use the SOFTWARE. The SOFTWARE is protected by copyright laws and international copyright treaties, as well as other intellectual property laws and treaties. The SOFTWARE is licensed, not sold.

1. GRANT OF LICENSE.

The SOFTWARE is licensed for use on one computer.

2. DESCRIPTION OF OTHER RIGHTS AND LIMITATIONS.

a. You must not remove or alter any copyright notices on any and all copies of the SOFTWARE.
b. You may not distribute registered copies of the SOFTWARE to third parties.
c. You may not reverse engineer, decompile, or disassemble the SOFTWARE.
d. You may not rent, lease, or lend the SOFTWARE.
e. You must comply with all applicable laws regarding use of the SOFTWARE.

3. TERMINATION

Without prejudice to any other rights, Company may terminate this EULA if you fail to comply with the terms and conditions of this EULA. In such event, you must return or destroy all copies of the SOFTWARE in your possession.

4. COPYRIGHT

All title, including but not limited to copyrights, in and to the SOFTWARE and any copies thereof are owned by Company. All title and intellectual property rights in and to the content which may be accessed through use of the SOFTWARE is the property of the respective content owner and may be protected by applicable copyright or other intellectual property laws and treaties. This EULA grants you no rights to use such content. All rights not expressly granted are reserved by Company.

5. NO WARRANTIES

The SOFTWARE is provided "As Is" without any express or implied warranty of any kind, including but not limited to any warranties of merchantability, no infringement, or fitness of a particular purpose. Company does not warrant or assume responsibility for the accuracy or completeness of any information, text, graphics, links or other items contained within the SOFTWARE. Company makes no warranties respecting any harm that may be caused by the transmission of a computer virus, worm, time bomb, logic bomb, or other such computer program.

6. LIMITATION OF LIABILITY

In no event shall Company be liable for any damages (including, without limitation, lost profits, business interruption, or lost information) rising out of "Authorized Users" use of or inability to use the SOFTWARE, even if Company has been advised of the possibility of such damages. In no event will Company be liable for loss of data or for indirect, special, incidental, consequential (including lost profit), or other damages based in contract, tort or otherwise. Company shall have no liability with respect to the content of the SOFTWARE or any part thereof, including but not limited to errors or omissions contained therein, libel, infringements of rights of publicity, privacy, trademark rights, business interruption, personal injury, loss of privacy, moral rights or the disclosure of confidential information.

7. OPEN SOURCE LICENSE NOTICES

The following are notices compliant with software libraries included in this product.

Log4j, Google Data Java Client, Google Guava Library, Android V-Card, Soap, XMLBeans, OpenCSV, HTTPComponents, HttpClient are licensed under the Apache Software License, Version 2.0 www.apache.org/licenses/LICENSE-2.0

Mozilla Libraries , Saxon, and IcePDF are licensed under the Mozilla Public License MPL v2.0 https://www.mozilla.org/en-US/MPL/2.0/

JavaMail: is licensed from Oracle JavaMail(TM) API 1.4.3 www.java.com/en/download/license.jsp

Appframework, DJNativeSwing, JNA and Beansbinding are licensed under the GNU Lesser General Public License 2.1 LGPL-2.1 www.opensource.org/licenses/lgpl-2.1.php, Source code available at www.telikin.com/open_source.php

TinyCore Linux, the Linux kernel, and various other binaries distributed on this product are licensed under the GNU General Public License Version 2 GPL v2 www.gnu.org/licenses/gpl-2.0.html, Source code available at www.telikin.com/open_source.php

LibreOffice Libraries are licensed under the GNU Lesser General Public Library LGPL v3 www.opensource.org/licenses/lgpl-3.0, Source code available at www.telikin.com/open_source.php

JXLayer, TimingFramework, and AnimatedTransitions are licensed under the BSD License. www.freebsd.org/copyright/license.html

XStream: BSD License Copyright (c) 2003-2006, Joe Walnes, Copyright (c) 2006-2007, XStream Committers All rights reserved.

- Redistribution and use in source and binary forms, with or without modification, are permitted provided that the following conditions are met:
- Redistributions of source code must retain the above copyright notice, this list of conditions and the following disclaimer. Redistributions in binary form must reproduce the above copyright notice, this list of conditions and the following disclaimer in the documentation and/or other materials provided with the distribution.
- Neither the name of XStream nor the names of its contributors may be used to endorse or promote products derived from this software without specific prior written permission.

THIS SOFTWARE IS PROVIDED BY THE COPYRIGHT HOLDERS AND CONTRIBUTORS "AS IS" AND ANY EXPRESS OR IMPLIED WARRANTIES, INCLUDING, BUT NOT LIMITED TO, THE IMPLIED WARRANTIES OF MERCHANTABILITY AND FITNESS FOR A PARTICULAR PURPOSE ARE DISCLAIMED. IN NO EVENT SHALL THE COPYRIGHT OWNER OR CONTRIBUTORS BE LIABLE FOR ANY DIRECT, INDIRECT, INCIDENTAL, SPECIAL, EXEMPLARY, OR CONSEQUENTIAL DAMAGES (INCLUDING, BUT NOT LIMITED TO, PROCUREMENT OF SUBSTITUTE GOODS OR SERVICES; LOSS OF USE, DATA, OR PROFITS; OR BUSINESS INTERRUPTION) HOWEVER CAUSED AND ON ANY THEORY OF LIABILITY, WHETHER IN CONTRACT, STRICT LIABILITY, OR TORT (INCLUDING NEGLIGENCE OR OTHERWISE) ARISING IN ANY WAY OUT OF THE USE OF THIS SOFTWARE, EVEN IF ADVISED OF THE POSSIBILITY OF SUCH DAMAGE.

Xpp3: Version 1.1.1 www.extreme.indiana.edu/xgws/xsoap/xpp/ Copyright (c) 2002 Extreme! Lab, Indiana University. All rights reserved. "This product includes software developed by the Indiana University Extreme! Lab www.extreme.indiana.edu" THIS SOFTWARE IS PROVIDED "AS IS" AND ANY EXPRESSED OR IMPLIED WARRANTIES, INCLUDING, BUT NOT LIMITED TO, THE IMPLIED WARRANTIES OF MERCHANTABILITY AND FITNESS FOR A PARTICULAR PURPOSE ARE DISCLAIMED. IN NO EVENT SHALL THE AUTHORS, COPYRIGHT HOLDERS OR ITS CONTRIBUTORS BE LIABLE FOR ANY DIRECT, INDIRECT, INCIDENTAL, SPECIAL, EXEMPLARY, OR CONSEQUENTIAL DAMAGES (INCLUDING, BUT NOT LIMITED TO, PROCUREMENT OF SUBSTITUTE GOODS OR SERVICES; LOSS OF USE, DATA, OR PROFITS; OR BUSINESS INTERRUPTION) HOWEVER CAUSED AND ON ANY THEORY OF LIABILITY, WHETHER IN CONTRACT, STRICT LIABILITY, OR TORT (INCLUDING NEGLIGENCE OR OTHERWISE) ARISING IN ANY WAY OUT OF THE USE OF THIS SOFTWARE, EVEN IF ADVISED OF THE POSSIBILITY OF SUCH DAMAGE.

ICal4J: Copyright (c) 2011, Ben Fortuna All rights reserved. Redistribution and use in source and binary forms, with or without modification, are permitted provided that the following conditions are met:

Java Pdf Extraction Decoding Access Library:

Project Info: http://www.jpedal.org (C) Copyright 1997-2008, IDRsolutions and Contributors. Main Developer: Simon Barnett

Other JBIG2 image decoding implementations include jbig2dec (http://jbig2dec.sourceforge.net/) xpdf (http://www.foolabs.com/xpdf/)

The final draft JBIG2 specification can be found at http://www.jpeg.org/public/fcd14492.pdf

All three of the above resources were used in the writing of this software, with methodologies, processes and inspiration taken from all three.

Java Pdf CCITTFax Decoding Library:

Based on the SUN code (see license beyond) changes are made to handle CCITTFax encoded data in a PDF image. This may or may not apply to real world CCITT documents.

Save Your Account Information

Network
   Wireless Network Name (SSID): _____

   Wireless Network Password:_____

Email
   Email Address:_____

   Email Password:_____

Photos (Facebook)
   Facebook Email Address:_____

   Facebook Password:_____

_____Username:_____

_____Password:_____

_____Username:_____

_____Password:_____

_____Username:_____

_____Password:_____

_____Username:_____

_____Password:_____

_____Username:_____

_____Password:_____

Returns & Warranty Replacement Information

Thank you for your purchase! We take every effort to ensure that your merchandise arrives in excellent condition. For your satisfaction, we offer a 60-day, unconditional return policy and a 1-year equipment warranty.

Return Policy

If, for whatever reason, you are not satisfied with your purchase, you may return it for a refund (excludes shipping). In order to receive a full refund, returned items must comply with the following terms:

- **You must call to receive a Return Authorization (RA) number**
- All items must be returned within 60 days of purchase
- Returned item(s) must be returned in "factory fresh" condition
- Returned item(s) must be returned in original packaging

Please save your boxes and packing materials! Returns with missing parts will be subject to the following restocking fees:

Keyboard: $19   Mouse: $10   Power Supply: $75   Box: $3   Internal Packing: $15

Instructions for Return

1. **Call 1-800-730-6893 to get a Return Authorization (RA) number.**
2. Complete the form on the next page and include it in your return, for your own records, also record the RA# below.
3. When packing your return, include all items in their original boxes (**you do not need to return your User Manual**). Packing instructions are located on page 14 of this User Manual.
4. When you call for the return, our Customer Support Agent will schedule a UPS Pickup for you with a Return Shipping Label

Instructions for Warranty Replacement

1. **Call 1-800-730-6893 to get a Warranty Replacement Authorization (WRA) number.**
2. When you call, we will provide a label and arrange for UPS to pickup your warranty item. Let us know if you do not have original boxes and/or packing materials.
3. When packing your warranty item, include all items in their original boxes (**you do not need to return your User Manual**). Packing instructions are located on page 14 of this User Manual.

Venture 3 Systems
RA#_____
2805 Sterling Drive
Hatfield, PA 19440

Telikin Return Form

Wait! If you are having any issues, setting up your computer, connecting to the internet, getting your email, or enjoying your Telikin in any way, CALL US at 1-800-730-6893, we can help!

Our Support hours are Monday-Friday, 8am-8pm, Saturday, 10am-6pm and Sunday, 11:30am-7:30pm, Eastern Time

If you still wish to return your Telikin Computer:

Call 1-800-730-6893 for an RA# to avoid restocking fees, or delays with your refund!

Follow the instructions on the previous page, then...

Please detach and include this form in the box with your return. Failing to return this form will significantly delay the processing of your refund.

Return Authorization (RA) # _____

Name: _____

Address: _____

_____

Reason for Return: Check as many as applicable

☐ Could not get connected to the Internet
☐ Need more Features (Please explain in comments below)
☐ Health Related; vision, dexterity, etc.
☐ Other (Please explain in comments below)

Comments: _____

_____

_____

_____

VIP Support 800-730-6893
New Customers 800-730-6893
Standard Support 267-954-0110

A simpler, easy to use computer.

AIO Rev #3.5.6
20200624

Copyright 2020 • Venture 3 Systems LLC. • Hatfield, PA

Made in the USA
Middletown, DE
15 July 2024